HUSTLE AND HAVE FUN!

"Hustle and Have Fun! is a positive and refreshing approach to teaching youth sports. If you're a coach or a parent, read this book!"
Gregg Popovich, Head Coach/President San Antonio Spurs
Coach of five NBA Championship teams, winningest coach in NBA history, and longest tenured active coach in professional sports

"Coach Gutterman gets to the heart of coaching in "Hustle and Have Fun!" His seven points are the essence of why we coach. I wholeheartedly agree with using this book as your blueprint for coaching!"
Don MacAdam, Former Assistant Coach Detroit Red Wings
Forty-plus years of global coaching experience in the NHL, AHL, ECHL, OHL, QMJHL, Japan, and Europe

"Hustle and Have Fun" is an entertaining read and useful tool for coaches at every level. I highly recommend it to all coaches and aspiring coaches."
Frank Serratore, Head Hockey Coach, Air Force Academy
Coach of nine championship teams (USHL, IHL, NCAA) and USA Hockey's U-17 developmental team

"This is a must-read for any current or aspiring coach. In "Hustle and Have Fun!" General Gutterman has captured a great insight: character and values are essential for success in all aspects of your life. This book is really something special, Bravo!"
Brian Raduenz, CEO AVEX Aerospace

"Highly recommend anyone involved in youth athletics, from coaches to parents, read this book. I even found Coach's insights relevant to my board room -- this is a great book!"
Stephen Chambal, Former CEO / Co-Founder, The Perduco Group

"What a beautiful piece of work! A "must read" for all youth teachers, coaches, players, parents and people in leadership positions. Coach Gutt hit the nail on the head!"
Byron Glime, United States Navy (Retired)
Father of five with thirty-eight grandchildren -- youth sports observer for seventy-plus years

HUSTLE & HAVE FUN!

A Coach's Guide to Winning Over Players and Parents

Coach Greg Gutterman
Brigadier General, United States Air Force, Retired

Gutt Check Series
Greg Gutterman Group (G3) Publication

Copyright © 2022 by Greg Gutterman. All Rights Reserved. No part of this publication may be reproduced, copied, stored, distributed, or used in any manner without prior written permission.

Greg Gutterman Group, LLC
P.O Box 94
Alpha, OH 45301
CoachGutt@hustleandhave.fun

LIBRARY OF CONGRESS CATALOG-IN-PRINTING DATA
Gutterman, Gregory 1966 -
 Hustle and Have Fun! A Coach's Guide to Winning Over Players and Parents by Greg Gutterman. -- 1st ed.

ISBN: 979-8-9869443-0-2 (ebook) | ISBN: 979-8-9869443-1-9 (paperback) | 979-8-9869443-2-6 (hardcover)

1. Sports for Children--coaching. 2. Youth Sports--Coaching. 3. Winter Sports. 4. Sports and Outdoors. 5. Hockey. 6. Non-Fiction - Self Help. 7. Ice Skating. 8. Children's and Youth Sports. 9. Training. 10. Teen and Young Adult.

Cover photo courtesy of Judi Morrissey Photography
Cover design by The Next Wave, LLC
First Edition. Printed in the United States of America

The views expressed in this publication are those of the author and do not necessarily reflect the official policy or position of the Department of Defense or the U.S. government. The public release clearance of this publication by the Department of Defense does not imply Department of Defense endorsement or factual accuracy of the material.

Special Note from the Author

A portion of the proceeds from this book will be donated to the not-for-profit Academy Hockey Club (academyhockey.org). The Academy's mission is to increase participation and diversity in the sport of ice hockey. The Academy accomplishes its mission by providing free learn-to-skate and learn-to-play opportunities for young athletes. Thank you for supporting the Academy by purchasing this book.

In honor of my three life passions: my family, my Air Force, and my student-athletes.

Table of Contents

Preface i

Introduction 1

First: Remain Player-Centric 9

Second: Don't Worry About the Scoreboard 15

Third: Manage Expectations 27

Fourth: Act Like the Role Model You Are 39

Fifth: Treat the Parents Like Adults 45

Sixth: Run Balanced Practices 55

Seventh: Treat Games as Your Primary Classroom . 63

Conclusion 77

Afterword 85

Appendix A: Coaching Commitment 91

Appendix B: Playbook 97

Appendix C: Videos and Books 101

Bibliography 105

Acknowledgments 107

Upcoming Books and Contact Information 108

About the Author 109

Preface

When I was ten years old I played a Little League baseball game at a field about a block away from my childhood home. I walked to the field with my mom and dad, and as I joined my teammates on the field, my parents took a seat in the bleachers behind the third base dugout. They had a perfect view of the performance I was about to give.

I walked up to the plate for my first at bat, and struck out. I was embarrassed and angry. In my frustration I hurled the bat toward the dugout and kicked at the dirt hard scattering small pebbles and dust into the air.

Two innings later I stepped back up to the plate to redeem myself, but instead registered another 'K' in the scorebook. Two at bats, two strikeouts.

My frustration turned into a full-on tirade. I flung my bat toward the dugout nearly missing my teammate who was on deck to hit next. I launched my helmet so forcefully it hit the back-stop fencing right in front of my mortified parents in the stands. On the way back to the players' bench, I kicked the dirt so vigorously I momentarily disappeared in a cloud of dust. What a performance!

Two acts remained in the game. My third trip to the plate, the bat connected solidly and sent the ball out of the park for a home run. My fourth and final at bat I sent the ball well over the left-field fence for my second home run. I was proud of myself.

After the game I confidently joined my parents for the short walk home. Once we were out of ear-shot of others, my dad asked me how I felt I had played. I said, "Great! I hit .500 with two homers!"

"Yes, Gregory, you did. But the only thing people will remember about the game is how you acted when you struck out," my dad replied.

My dad taught me a valuable life lesson that day: you cannot let your frustrations or emotions take control of your behavior. Instead of acting childish and defeated, take a deep breath and try harder the next time. I played in that Little-League baseball game well over forty years ago, and although I can't remember if our team won or lost that day, I remember my dad's lesson like it was yesterday. That is the staying power of a true-life lesson.

The lessons learned playing youth sports provided me a solid foundation from which to build my life. Traits like teamwork, discipline, self-belief, loyalty, grit, humility, respect, work ethic, and more, became part of my character because I played baseball, football, and ice hockey growing up. These life skills have lifted me to personal and professional successes well beyond what the bat-throwing little-leaguer could have ever imagined. I am forever grateful.

It was my recognition, in fact, of the role being a student-athlete played in my character development, that ultimately led me to become a coach myself over thirty years ago. Sports built the character-based foundation for who I am and what I have in life, and I continue to have a driving desire to give back to youth sports as a result. Coaching provides me the honor and opportunity to teach these same character traits to my players, so they have a solid footing from which to build their own amazing lives.

Three decades of coaching lessons have been winnowed into this purposefully short read. I consider this book a starting point or blueprint for the rookie youth coach, or the

PREFACE

veteran coach looking to improve, or maybe even find a reason to continue coaching.

I want every youth coach to recognize how critically important they are to teaching lifelong traits and skills through sports. The types of lessons that allow a player, through hard work and determination, to become the best versions of themselves possible in both sports and life.[1] This is my passionate purpose and the reason I wrote this book.

On the fields of friendly strife are sown the seeds that on other days, on other fields, will bear the fruits of victory.[2]
General Douglas MacArthur

Endnotes

1   My abbreviated version of legendary Coach John Wooden's definition of success. See *Wooden: A lifetime of Observations and Reflections On and Off the Court*. This book is cited in the appendix and bibliography.

2   During Basic Cadet Training at the United States Air Force Academy, Cadets are issued a copy of *Contrails*. The small but thick index sized book contains leadership quotes, military history, and weapon system facts. My copy was issued to me in 1985. This book is cited in the appendix and bibliography.

Introduction

I was seven years old and the temperature outside our modest Minnesota home matched my age. "Boys put on your coats and snow pants, we're going to the park to skate," Dad said as he stepped inside the house after work that night.

Dad normally came home from work, sat down in his reclining chair, kicked off his boots, and relaxed. But not tonight. Tonight he was taking his boys to the park to play. It didn't matter how dark and cold it was outside. It didn't matter that it was well past dinner-time. All that mattered was Dad wanted to go to the park with his boys and have some fun.

Despite the dark hour and frigid temperatures, Mom didn't object. She had another day like the preceding ones. A "Boys, you just wait 'til your dad gets home" kind of day. As soon as Dad told us to get ready for the park, Mom was already opening a bottle of Sangria and moving toward the couch.

My mom was understandably exhausted. By the time they celebrated their third anniversary, three baby boys were in the mix. The final attempt to add a girl to the family line-up resulted in another boy batting clean-up. Four boys under the age of eight, trapped inside a house in the middle of a cold Minnesota winter's day, would exhaust anyone.

About a block away from my childhood home was a baseball field that doubled for an outdoor ice rink in the winter. Once the cold weather came in, the firemen opened a hydrant near the park and flooded the area with layers and layers of water. They did this a few times a day, for about a week. When they were done dumping a ton of water onto the cold ground, a three-inch-deep frozen pond appeared.

Dad walked us to the outdoor rink and had us sit on a snowbank near the edge of the ice where he quickly swapped out our boots for pairs of light-blue, double-bladed, vinyl ice skates he had picked up at the store on the way home from work. We were excited to give it a go, but there was a problem: Dad didn't know how to skate. Instead of giving us instruction, he picked us up and pushed us forward. We fell one-by-one laughing at each other. Dad picked us up again and repeated the process over and over again, times four, until he pushed us, and we stayed upright. As Dad stretched out his aching back, he watched his four little laughing penguins walking on ice, and I saw him crack an elusive smile.

A few days later Mom bundled us up again, looked at me, and said, "Gregory, take your brothers to the park and skate. I'll call you home when lunch is ready."

Our city parks department had built a small cinderblock storage building at the baseball park. During summer break from school there were bats, balls, gloves, and more, available to check out. All the neighborhood kids would rally at the park every morning, all summer long, for some competitive day-long fun. In the winter the storage building became a warming shack, which could have doubled as a prison-cell, since it was built without windows and only a solitary bulb in the ceiling dimly lit the cement gray room.

My brothers and I walked around the block to the park and waved to Mom. Mom was watching us from our backyard deck which was within sight of the ice rink. After the salutations were exchanged, she disappeared inside to the

INTRODUCTION

warmth of the house while we did the same by entering the prison cell. My brothers and I quickly swapped out our snow boots for the light-blue double-bladed vinyl skates and stepped back outside onto the ice. All of our neighborhood friends were there, just like in the summer. It was a blast.

In the blink of an eye, we heard Mom calling us home, "Boys, lunch is ready!" We were having so much fun, we didn't want to be called home. We just wanted to keep playing in our version of Peter Pan's Neverland.

I relished going to the park in the wintertime. Every time I skated the wind raced across my face making me feel like I was flying. The snow muffled out every background noise leaving only laughter hanging in the air, and Mother Nature's wand had painted the surroundings a like-new white. There was so much fun and enjoyment being on the ice with my friends that I went to the park almost every single day in the winter. I simply loved it.

My passion for skating propelled me from those light-blue double-bladed skates into a pair of well-used "real" hockey skates by the end of my first winter skating. My parents must have seen the joy and passion I had for the sport because at the start of the next winter, they decided to sign me up for the local youth hockey program.

When the other parents heard I would be turning eight years old soon, was self-taught, and only had one winter of experience, they told my parents I was "late to the game" and would never catch up to the other players. I love a challenge like that to this day.

I wish I remembered my first coach's name because I owe him a debt of gratitude I can never repay. He propelled me from a late-to-the-game beginner to the top-tier of players in a single season. As a result, I made the "A" Squirt team the next winter and joined the top flock of under ten-year-old hockey players in my small blue-collar town.

During my entire youth playing career I had great coaches with incredible attention to detail, the ability to motivate, and a long-term vision of what each player could become. What a positive difference a good coach and your parents' belief and support make in sports and life. I was so lucky to have these role models growing up.

By the time I hit high school I could keep up with anyone in the state, made the varsity team's first line as a sophomore (freshmen were not allowed to play high school sports back then), and was named Captain of the team my senior season.

I was lucky enough (and perhaps good enough) to get noticed by an assistant ice hockey coach from the United States Air Force Academy. After a lengthy application process and six college entrance exams, I was finally qualified for, and admitted into, our Nation's Air Force Academy.

Looking back, I was more than lucky to get noticed and accepted into the Academy. The Academy was the only college I applied to, and I didn't know it at the time, but only 1,100 qualified high-school seniors are accepted each year.[3] It wasn't luck, it was divine intervention.

I played a total of eighty-four National Collegiate Athletic Association Division I hockey games at the Academy. What a ride! But just like that, four years had passed, my hockey career was ending, and graduation pending. Before either would come to pass, there was one more event remaining in my hockey career: the post-season team awards banquet.

During the social hour prior to the event, I was

reminiscing with my teammates about the pranks we got away with on the road, the games we won, and the ones we should have won. As we were laughing it up, in walked the keynote speaker for the evening: Coach Bob Johnson.

The legendary Bob Johnson. Coach Johnson delivered four National Championships to the University of Wisconsin, and a Stanley Cup Championship to the National Hockey League's Pittsburgh Penguins. Even the road leading to the United States youth hockey organization's headquarters in Colorado is named after him.

"It's a great day for hockey" was Coach Johnson's signature quote. Coach Johnson is a three-time Hall of Famer and a coaching legend, and here he was at our post-season hockey banquet. Wow!

After an unremarkable banquet dinner, it was time for Coach Johnson to speak. There is no doubt he had our undivided attention, especially mine. All these years later I remember exactly what he said, and how the long "Ohs" of this true Northern Minnesotan made us all feel at home.

> "Booyz, I just spent the day touring this incredible Air Force Academy. Wow, what a place! Did ya know, did ya know boys -- they spent a million dollars on your education? A million dollars on each of ya! Now I'm lookin' at cha, every one of ya, and I'm pretty confident I'm right on this one. Not a single one of ya got in here because of your academics. *(He paused as the room filled with laughter-based concurrence.)* The way I see it is, you got in here because you play hockey. Hockey gave you that million-dollar education. So I only have one question for each of ya: how will you give back to the game of hockey, for all it gave to you?"

Coach Johnson was one-hundred percent on-target about the Academy Hockey Team's number twenty-three, Greg Gutterman, that night. Hockey was the singular reason I found out about the Academy, applied, and was accepted. Soon I would be graduating with a college degree in engineering and a guaranteed job as a commissioned officer on the greatest military team on the planet. Hockey truly did give me a million-dollar education. But even more, hockey gave me a million-dollar life opportunity. I made up my mind right then and there: I'll give back to hockey for giving me a million-dollar education, by becoming a coach.

A few short years after graduating from the Academy, the Air Force sent me to Ohio, where I met my wife, you guessed it, at the local ice rink. Today we are twenty-seven years strong, blessed with three incredible children, and have retired from the Air Force after a successful thirty-year active-duty career. The blessings I enjoy to this very day are rooted in the fact my dad decided to give my mom a break, and took his boys to the outdoor ice rink to skate.

I have spent over three-decades making good on the unspoken answer I gave to Coach Johnson's challenge. I have coached in North Dakota, Utah, Virginia, Kansas, Florida, and Ohio. I've coached three-year-old soccer players up to twenty-four-year-old college hockey players. Every season, and every team, I worked to do two simple things: make a positive impact on my players and my team, and keep improving as their coach.

This intentionally short book captures seven essential recommendations I refined during my three-decades of coaching youth sports. I document them here to help the rookie youth coach, or veteran youth coach, be successful

INTRODUCTION

from the start. I have no doubt my simple coaching blueprint will help you win over the players and their parents.

Endnotes

3 The Academy only accepts eleven percent of academically eligible candidates each year making it extremely selective. I ultimately served in the military for three-decades, and retired as a Brigadier General. It was the defining honor of my lifetime. But that's a story for another day.

First: Remain Player-Centric

Focus on what is in the best interest of the players

I made the top-tier "A" team from age eight to twelve growing up playing hockey in Minnesota. In my fifth season I was cut to the "B" team at tryouts. A quick scan of the before and after rosters highlighted the fact I was the only player demoted that year. All of my good friends and teammates remained on the "A" team ahead of me.

I was hurt, embarrassed, and wondered how I could keep playing. Somehow in my thirteen-year-old shocked state, I gathered the moral courage to ask the coach why I didn't make the top team.

"Gutt, you have the skill and speed. But you are not ready for the physical side of the game yet at this level. You will get more playing time and develop more as a player on the B-team. I'm confident this will make you a better overall player" the coach said.

My parents talked to the coach too, and they heard the same reasoning with one addition. The coach told my parents, "Greg can be a great player someday if he wants to do the work it requires to become one. This is something he can do on his own, irrespective of playing on the A or B team."

When my dad finished telling me what the coach had said, he finished by saying "If you want to make the A team next year, it's there for the taking. You can use this experience to fuel your fire, or to quit. That choice is yours."

The downgrade pushed me to put in more effort on and off the ice. I was one hundred percent committed and motivated to earn my way back onto the A-team the following season. As a B-teamer I became the leading scorer and biggest threat to every opponent we faced. In practices I worked to be the fastest in every drill no matter how tired I was, and I went to as many of the A-team games as I could to support my friends. When the season ended, I was proud of the fact I followed my dad's advice and used the disappointment to ignite my desire for focused improvement.

Before I knew it my B-team season had ended and the Minnesota snow was giving way to spring. Day by day I walked to and from school watching the ice slowly melt on my beloved outdoor rink. It first became slush, then a shallow pond, and finally a 17,000-square-foot puddle of mud. That's when I noticed that sunk deep into the mud were two, four-by-six-foot steel fenced abandoned hockey nets. I called a friend, and within an hour one of the rusted hockey nets was in my parents' single-car garage, mud and all!

All spring and summer long my friend and I shot pucks. Hundreds of shots became thousands. We invented new games to introduce competition and keep the time in the garage fun and interesting. First to hit the four corners and fastest to snipe thirty shots became my favorite games. My friend enjoyed goalie war using tennis balls because he won that game every time (turns out I am a terrible goalie).

At my mom's insistence we even learned how hard it was to repair the holes and dents in the garage walls that resulted from our wayward shots. After which, we focused harder on hitting the net, and just to be safe, we nailed old sheets and blankets from the garage rafters to stop our inaccurate snipes from doing further damage.

By the next season, I was a different player. Faster, stronger, more skilled, and significantly tougher mentally. I gained more confidence and captured a much better work ethic. As a result, I made the A-team's first line at age 14 and every season thereafter.

My player-centric coach was one hundred percent correct: I developed more as a B-team player than I ever would have as an A-team player. Thank you coach for giving me the nudge I needed to take personal responsibility and start working to become my very best!

The lesson I learned all those years ago is now a frequently repeated phrase I tell my players. **The small efforts toward improvement, consistently applied day in and day out, will reap tremendous lifetime rewards**. The muddy and rusted hockey net in our garage was my daily reminder to bring my personal best effort, both physically and mentally, to every undertaking.

I have found as a coach that there is no higher sense of satisfaction than watching a student-athlete go from *I can't* to *I can't yet* to *I can* and ultimately, *I did*. The players will carry this process and mindset of continual improvement and self-belief with them throughout their entire lives. This helps create people of character, and it is why coaching is such a vital voluntary profession.

Each February I hold a Senior Banquet for my graduating high-school hockey players. I think it is important for the coaches to recognize and honor the players who helped make the program better than they found it. The players who build and sustain a culture of excellence where doing your ultimate best is the measure of success, not a scoreboard.

I remind the Seniors several times before the banquet they will be required to give a short speech after the dinner. I also tell them, "If you only say one thing, make sure it is to thank your mom and dad." Being grateful for all the time, energy, and money your parents have sacrificed so you can play the sport is important. In my opinion, gratitude and humility are at the top of the list of admirable qualities in any human being.

Public speaking is also an essential life skill and our tradition helps (or in some cases forces) a few of our seniors to get out of their shells a little. The primary objective of the speeches, however, is for our Seniors to let their teammates know what playing for this team has meant to them. Every year this event gets more and more emotional for me.

A few seasons ago, as my son was giving his senior speech, I caught tears welling up in my eyes but I held them back. A few seasons later the tear ducts let loose during one of our senior's speeches.

He started his talk with "I'm not gonna cry," and within a few minutes, the entire room was in some form of a hand-to-cheek wiping motion. In this Senior's final speech, and during his short time to talk, he first thanked his parents. Then he shared a few funny stories before looking at one of his life-long teammates, our senior goalie. As they exchanged eye contact, he thanked him for being such a good teammate, a friend, a brother.

Then he looked at his fifteen other teammates and told them how much he loved them. Yes, a High School Senior used the word love. As he talked, he started to pause in between words to let the tears slowly drop from his eyes and to recapture enough composure to keep talking.

He finished by thanking the coaches. With tears free-falling from his eyes, we heard, "I have never been on a team where the coaches believed in me so much. Never." Then he turned toward where I was sitting, and asked, "Can I get a hug, coach?" I am tearing up just thinking about this story, still humbled and honored by the validation this provided me as his coach.

I wanted to share these two particular stories with you to highlight a stark contrast. On one hand my youth coach had to cut me to the "B" team to inspire my improvement and teach me a valuable life lesson on giving your personal best effort in all you do. On the other hand, my senior needed to know his coach believed in him, so he could in turn learn the importance of believing in himself. Both stories have the same main point: **a player-centric coach puts what is in the best interest of the player's long-term growth and development above all else**. This, not a single game, season, or scoreboard, is what being a player-centric coach is all about.

Second: Don't Worry About the Scoreboard

Focus on the life skills and traits that will sustain the players well after their playing days are done

When I was fourteen years old my hockey team played an away game against a league opponent we had beaten by ten goals earlier in the season. Although my team was projected to win by that amount again, we ended the first two periods of play tied up at 0 to 0. My teammates and I were matching our opponent's pace of play, instead of playing at our own.

My coach didn't lose his mind screaming and yelling. Instead, after the second period, he simply pulled the goalie.[4] That's right, with a full fifteen-minute third period to go in the contest, my coach pulled our team's goalie from the game giving our less skilled opponents a clear advantage: an unprotected goal cage. We were startled, horrified, and in disbelief. As I am sure you can imagine, so were the parents in the stands.

Then we heard Coach say, in a loud but calm voice so everyone would hear it, "if you are not going to play your best, then they deserve to win. I suggest you start working together and play your best, or they will." We stepped up to our level of play and won the game.

The lesson I learned that day from our great coach was

that **it never matters who you play, it only matters how you play**. You should always play to the best of your abilities. Nothing more, nothing less. This is how you succeed, win, lose, or tie.

Decades later I was coaching an under ten-year-old coed hockey team. We had only a few weekly fifty-minute practices before facing off in our first game. We lost 0 to 7. The players were dejected and the parents were upset. But I was neither. Now don't get me wrong, I hate losing like everyone else. But I truly believed the players did their ultimate best and kept fighting to the end despite the lopsided scoreboard. That's a successful game in my coaching mind.

After the game, an awesome assistant coach took me aside. "Gutt, we may want to spend some time teaching positioning before our next game," he said.

I thanked him for the honest feedback, which is essential if you want to improve as a coach. In fact, **to be an effective coach you have to be approachable and receive feedback (even brutally honest feedback) without becoming defensive or emotional**. My assistant highlighted the fact that up to that point in time, I had only included players' skills development in my practice plans. As a result, our young players had not practiced any team plays or positioning before the first game.

He was correct, I was singularly focused on skills development for our young team. I told him, "My opinion is we won't be able to do anything as a team if the kids can't skate, stickhandle, pass or shoot well." That is why I used our infrequent but invaluable ice-time on skills development. I finished by saying, "But don't worry, it will work out."

My assistant's honest feedback reminded me how important it is for the coach to keep everyone informed, including the parents. **The parents are essential to player growth and development, because the student-athlete will learn faster when all the adults in their lives are rowing together.** This is such an important point that I dedicated an entire chapter to parental interaction later in this book.

I put together an ad-hoc post-game team meeting so I could let everyone (players, parents, and assistants) know what I would be focusing on during the season. After everyone was assembled I said this.

> "Now, you may not like this, but the scoreboard is not how we'll define success this year. Instead, when the season is over, I am going to ask each player two questions, and our mutual success will be measured by how many players answer 'yes' to them.
>
> One: did you have fun this year? And two: are you going to play again next year? I believe we can get to "yes" on both questions by focusing on the Two H's: *Hustle* and *Have Fun*! This is all we should be asking of them this season in my opinion. After all, what good is winning if half the kids quit the sport after the season is over, because they did not have fun?"

Thankfully everyone agreed and we worked together to achieve these simple goals. Before every game and practice we emphasized the *Two H's* and the coaches doubled down on skill-focused practices. The players thrived in this environment and even made it to the championship game during the playoffs that season. But more importantly, I received a "yes'" to my two questions from every player on the team during our end-of-season pizza party. A successful season by any measure.

The *Two H's* are foundational to my overall coaching philosophy. The word *hustle* has many definitions, but what it means to me is to give your personal best effort in pursuit of a goal or objective.[5] In my opinion, **all you can ever ask of someone is for them to work hard and bring their best effort to a task.** This is something I learned from my mother during a visit back home while on leave from my military obligations many years ago.

My brothers, Mom, and I were talking after lunch one day, and at one point during the conversation the laughter turned to silence. I must have unintentionally made Mom upset because she used my full name as she began speaking. "Gregory, your father and I did the best we could, with what we knew, and what we had at the time," she said. Amen, Mom, you did and thank you!

We all have physical, mental, and other limitations or constraints. All we can do is our personal best with what we have and what we know: nothing more, nothing less. By doing so, we can achieve our own individual versions of success. The word hustle is my way of summarizing this essential thought process.

The word hustle also encapsulates associated life traits, skills, and habits like grit, teamwork, discipline, and much more. These are the traits of successful people and teams, yet they are elusive to measure. Quite simply, a scoreboard cannot gauge what it truly takes to become successful as a person, let alone a team. **An effective coach focuses on bringing out the personal best effort from their players (and team) rather than worrying about the scoreboard**. This is what the old saying "You can lose in a win, and win in a loss" truly means. The quote I like to use quite often to make the same point is, "Good things happen when you hustle."

There are three important character traits effective coaches should help their players build. Bringing forth their personal best effort is the first. Without hustle or effort, there can be no growth, improvement, or learning.

The second lifelong character trait effective coaches nurture is self-confidence or self-belief.

I had the habit of asking my children three questions at the dinner table each night when they were younger. Did you have fun today? What did you learn? And, how did you help your mom? One evening my youngest daughter could not wait for her turn to tell me what she had learned.

> "Daddy, today I learned if you say 'I can't' your brain turns off. But if you say 'I can't yet' it stays on."

I was wowed! My five-year-old daughter learned an essential life lesson from her Kindergarten teacher that day. So simple, isn't it? Adding the word 'yet' changes the entire thought process, and along with it, the person's entire attitude. Instead of saying, "I'm not good in math," so I quit, you now hear "I'm not good in math, yet," I'll keep working at it, I can do this, I'll get there.[6] In its simplicity you can see its brilliance.

As Henry Ford said decades ago, if you believe you can or can't, you're right. I see this phenomenon quite often while teaching young kids to skate as a voluntary instructor for a local not-for-profit organization. Every session there is a young person who steps on the ice, slips and falls. I show them how to get back up and try again. Soon enough they fall again, and as they lay on the ice I hear, "I can't."

Rather than confirm or reject the new skater's belief, I

simply ask them to add a word to the statement. "Barb, next time you think "I can't" can you add a word for me? Can you add the word, "yet, I can't...yet." By the end of the hour, they are marching on the ice without help.

A person's attitude and self-belief affect their entire life. "I can't" or "I quit" can creep into academics, professions, relationships and more. This negative attitude can, and most likely will, affect your players' entire lifetime. This is why it is so critically important for a coach to focus on enhancing players' self-belief, and similarly, belief in their teammates.

An effective coach teaches their players self-belief by recognizing and praising a player's (or a team's) effort in pursuit of a goal or objective, regardless of the result. By doing so you are validating the effort-to-improvement learning process, and the player's self-belief will follow. Here are a few examples of statements you can make to help embolden this "can do" attitude.

> That's how we hustle!
>
> Excellent, you moved to the perfect spot for that pass!
>
> Wow, you were flying right there. You're faster than you think!
>
> Yes, yes, yes. That's how we compete!
>
> I'm proud of you!

Some tips to help you control negative thoughts and emotions are provided later in this book. For now, remember that the second important character trait an effective coach teaches their players, is to believe in themselves.

The final trait effective coaches focus on inculcating in their players is good old-fashioned grit. Gritty players have a never-quit determination and unyielding motivation to work toward their personal goals and objectives despite all obstacles. In fact, researchers have concluded grit, not intellect, is the key factor in personal achievement,[7] and this should come as no surprise to any adult athlete or coach.

Several seasons ago my high school team was pitted against a statistically stronger team in the opening round of the state playoffs. A quick scan of the players' benches would confirm the pre-game expectations of a lopsided defeat: our bench had a scant twelve players, theirs a whopping twenty.

The game started with the ice tilted against us as bouncing pucks, weird deflections, and own goals put us behind 0 to 3 after one period of play. This was not what my seniors expected, or the last memory I wanted them to have of their competitive playing careers.

During the first period intermission every nose in the locker room was pointed at the floor and you could have heard a pin drop. The team was mentally defeated and we still had sixty-six percent of time remaining on the clock to compete, to fight, and to battle. I started my talk by asking them a few questions.

> "What kind of team do you want to have? Seniors, is this how you want to end your high school careers? Is this the culture you will leave behind or are you going to make it better than you found it? For everyone else, how do you want to finish the season for your Seniors?"

These were all open-ended and unanswered questions.

HUSTLE AND HAVE FUN!

The assistant coaches and I left the locker room to let the players think and talk among themselves about their answers. The main point I was making to the players was that this is their team, not the coaches. How they "go out" on the season, or their career as a Senior, is totally and one hundred percent up to them.

As we left the locker room for the second period, there was a new spark on the bench. The players' chins were up and their eyes were steeled. They had decided as a team that they were going to go out fighting to the end, regardless of the scoreboard. That is grit.

The second period started with both teams battling to avoid elimination. About halfway through the second period, we scored a goal and the players heard me repeating time and again "Keep working, everyone knows a two-goal lead is hard to keep."

Over and over again I repeated phrases like "Keep shooting, there is no such thing as a bad shot at this point." "Remember, great things happen when you hustle." And "Keep fighting, keep outworking them."

Five minutes later we scored again decreasing their lead to one, with the score our 2 goals to their 3. The second period ended, and the downward chins were now visibly seen on our opponent's bench, not ours.

The third period was a draw until, with around ten minutes remaining in the game, we scored to tie it up 3 to 3. Then a few minutes later we scored again to take a 4 to 3 lead. The parental pandemonium on our side of the stands wouldn't last, however, as our opponents matched the tally at four each and sent the game into sudden-death overtime.

The first overtime ended without a decision and the timekeepers put another fifteen minutes on the clock. Our

DON'T WORRY ABOUT THE SCOREBOARD

twelve skaters had competed against their twenty for a full hour of play already, and another overtime period was about to begin.

Despite being outnumbered and dehydrated, my team fought all the way to the bitter end, which came halfway through the second overtime when our opponents scored to win the game in double-overtime.

The scoreboard indicated we had lost the game, but the electronic lights couldn't measure the team's success that day. My crew was matched to a superior opponent, outnumbered, and down by three goals early in the game. Despite these high hurdles and obstacles, they continued to fight and compete to the very end. They simply never gave up and as a result they were one hundred percent successful in the eyes of every spectator and coach that day.

Success is so much more than winning. It is a level of personal contentment that comes from knowing, deep down, that you gave your personal best effort in pursuit of a goal or objective, for yourself and your teammates.[8, 9]

There are many more life traits and skills sports teach a player like discipline, teamwork, integrity, humility, and gratitude to name a few. These are important qualities for players to learn, no doubt. **But I contend teaching players to give their best personal effort, to believe in themselves, and to have a little grit are the traits that give rise to all others.** These are the three lifelong character traits effective coaches focus on rather than the scoreboard, because they are keys to your players' lifelong growth and development.

Endnotes

---

4   In ice hockey, "pulling" a goalie, means the goaltender moves to the players bench thereby vacating the goal. An extra skater or attacker is allowed on the ice instead.

5   The word hustle has twenty-two meanings per Dictionary.com. My use of the word expands on "energetic activity, as in work," and "to proceed or work rapidly and energetically."

6   This concept is known as *Mindset* and the title of a book by Dr. Carol Dweck. In her work Dr. Dweck found young students either see a problem an exciting opportunity, or insurmountable obstacle. She coined these two attitudes as either a growth mindset (I can't yet but I will try) or fixed mindset (I can't and I won't try). See the appendix for the full citation.

7   *Grit* is the title of a great book by Dr. Angela Duckworth. Her research focused on why some of the smartest children failed to succeed in difficult academic settings and situations. Her major finding was grit, or determined perseverance, not intellect, better determined future potential. See the appendix for the full citation.

8 I agree with legendary Coach John Wooden who said "Success is peace of mind which is a direct result of self-satisfaction in knowing you made the effort to become the best you are capable of becoming." See the appendix or bibliography for the full citation.

9 I encourage you to watch Coach John Wooden's *The Difference Between Winning and Succeeding;* Carol Dweck's *Mindset*; and Dr. Angela Duckworth's *Grit*. The videos are widely available online and cited in an appendix.

Third: Manage Expectations

A picture is worth a thousand words

My mom was a sports mom. She sat center ice or front row at almost every one of my games and was the loudest and most vocal cheerleader in the stands. The one thing I remember most about her when it comes to sports, though, was her way of reminding me simply and unambiguously to do my very best.

During my 1977 to 1978 youth hockey season, Mom hand-painted, glazed, and kiln-fired twenty ceramic mugs: one for each player and coach on my team. It was a labor of love and took her months to finish them all.

Every mug was as close to identical as Mom could make it. Around the body of the mug were all my teammates' names and jersey numbers, and to personalize each gift, she hand-painted a single player's (or coach's) name on the mug's handle.

On the front of every mug, in the central position, Mom hand-painted a small angry-faced hockey player, sticks, skates, gloves, and all. Above the hockey player she scribed "Winning isn't everything" and under the sketch, "wanting to is!"

Years later I learned this was a famous Vince Lombardi quote, but I will always consider it Mom's. It was her way of reminding all of us, in a clear and simple manner, to bring tireless effort to all we do. To battle. To compete.

That is how you became a winner in Mom's eyes.

Keeping it simple for your youth players is essential if you want them to learn enduring character traits. Like Mom's simple phrase, I have found using the words *battle*, *compete*, or *fight* requires players to bring out their best effort, display self-belief, and have a gritty determination. When a player competes in practices and games, they verify and validate the effort they have put in to improve their playing skills is paying off.

I had a player who was working on his shot off ice every day. I could see this improvement in practices, but in games he would be in a position to let his shot rip, and he'd forgo the shot to make a pass. I kept reminding him he'd put in a ton of effort to improve his shot, and it was time to trust it. During one game he was at the bottom of the offensive zone circle, let one rip, and scored!

This was a shot from a one-percent area of the ice, with a three-inch-by-three-inch area of opportunity above the goalie's shoulder. This goal was a spark like no other for this player. It was the validation during a game (*competition*) he needed to see how the work he put in (*effort*) to improve his shot (*skill*) had paid off (*belief*). As a result, this player doubled down on his off-ice shooting practice, especially after games where he did not perform as well as he expected of himself (*grit*).

I tell this particular story to highlight the cause-effect relationship between *effort* and *skills* improvement, and to demonstrate how *competition* enhances a player's *self-belief* and *grittiness*.[10] This understanding helped me create my model for teaching life sustaining character traits through sports and managing player and parent expectations along the way. I call it the **Gutt Check™**

MANAGE EXPECTATIONS

Performance Matrix, and it is my picture that is literally worth 1,000 words.

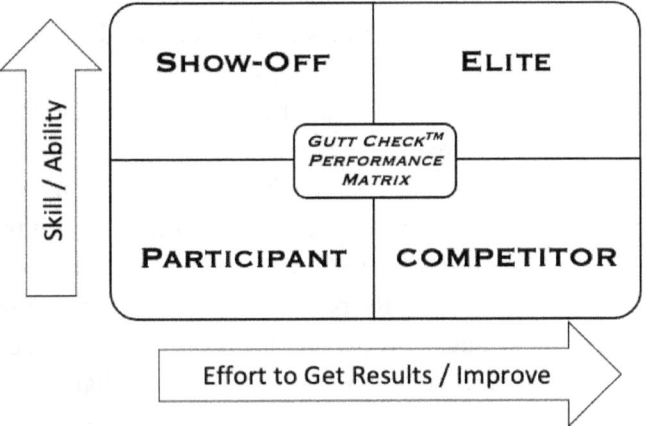

The Gutt Check Performance Matrix plots effort to improve or get results (cause) on the x-axis, and skill or ability (effect) on the y-axis. The matrix visually depicts the importance of my best-effort coaching philosophy and motivates the players' to seek all the benefits possible from bringing it.

The prerequisite for all improvement in sports and life is effort. Without effort there is no learning, no growth, no development. Period. This is why **effective coaches recognize, praise, and reward a player's (or a team's) effort in pursuit of improvement or results above all else**. Simple statements like "brilliant effort," "loved the hustle," "you can do it," and "keep working you're almost there" go a long way to motivating maximum effort from your players.

The second key matrix variable is skills improvement which is plotted along the y-axis. This is the validation a player receives their efforts are worth it, and as a result they begin to develop self-belief and grit. Coaches can provide positive reinforcement by using phrases like "Great shot," "Brilliant pass," and even "Much better" during games and practices to help spark players self-belief and determination.

Even negative outcomes can be used to form the basis for positive reinforcement. For example, after a goal is scored by an opponent, if a coach yells and screams at a player for making a mistake there is no learning. But if the coach says, "You did everything you could to take away time and space. Keep up the pace and they won't get another one." The latter statement changes the players' negative perspective, and refocuses them on working hard to "take away time and space." The main point is, even the smallest noticeable improvements should be praised by the coach to reinforce a players' effort is paying off.

Remember, the major focal point of the Performance Matrix is effort leads to improvement, improvement to self-belief, and self-belief to a gritty determination. This process all starts when **an effective coach praises a player's efforts in pursuit of their goals, while recognizing even the most subtle accomplishments.** Simply put, the Performance Matrix is a practical approach for teaching character through sports.

The Gutt Check Performance Matrix is also a great tool for managing expectations for players and parents. This done by physically plotting where a player is on the matrix with respect to their effort and associated skills improvement.

This visual referencing helps the coach (or player) perform a quick gut check on a players (or their) personal resolve, commitment, and priorities.[11] This process reinforces to your players that they are personally responsible and accountable for the amount of time and effort they invest into their own improvement. This is why the "10,000-hour rule" is something every coach should be teaching their players. [12]

The rule states it takes 10,000 hours of personal practice time to become your best at any activity (e.g. playing an instrument, getting a difficult degree, or becoming an elite athlete). Players who spend their free time playing video games instead of honing their athletic skills are indicating their priorities. This is fine in my book, as long as the video-game playing athlete (and their parents) have realistic expectations for their (or their child's) long-term prospects in the sport. **An effective coach sets and reinforces the expectation that players own one hundred percent of the personal effort and can-do attitude they bring to bear.** To become your best, you absolutely must put in the time and effort it takes to get there.

The Gutt-Check Performance Matrix has four quadrants purposefully named to enhance its influence as a powerful communication tool.

Participant (Low skill, Low Effort Players)

This is a social player, the one that is more interested in being associated with the team for friendships or ego purposes. Their misguided focus keeps them from putting in the effort required to become productive members of the team and work toward collective success.

As a coach you will recognize this type of player because of their "don't care" attitude during games, and/or lack of effort in formal and informal practices. They simply do not put in the personal effort to improve their skill levels.

The participant player also does not take personal responsibility for their growth and development, even after they are reminded their teammates deserve their personal best effort. If the participant player doesn't "get it," they should not be rewarded with much if any game time. You may even be forced to cut this type of player from you team to teach them an important life lesson: you are personally responsible and accountable for your actions, or inactions.

Show-Off (High Skill, Low Effort Player)

The show-off has natural God-given skills and abilities, but somewhere along the line developed a selfish attitude. Instead of helping everyone around them become better and bring the team to new heights, the show-off is more focused on their statistics and glory ahead of the team's success.

Motivating the show-off to develop a tireless work ethic and team-oriented attitude could result in them becoming an elite athlete; they certainly have the potential. But like all things in life, effort and attitude matter. Until the show-off "gets it" they too should see limited game time or even get cut from your team.

Remember, the ultimate focus of coaching youth players is not wins, records, and championships. The focus of coaching is to create people of character. Traits like effort and teamwork matter long-term, and this player needs to be taught these characteristics to become their personal best too.

Elite Performer (High Skill, High Effort Player)

Elite athletes have God-given talent, athleticism, and a tireless desire to improve. This stellar player is self-motivated and puts in the extra effort in games and practices to continually improve. Off-ice and off-season, they follow the 10,000-hour rule of personal practice to hone their abilities. One of the best compliments I can give to a player in this category, is they elevate the performance of everyone around them. They make their teammates better too.

Many players do not like to hear this, but truly elite athletes are few and far between. This is the top one to five percent of players who ultimately compete at the Division I college level, and in some cases become professional players in their respective sports.

Nonetheless, every player can become their personal best, an elite athlete by their own personal definition. This is the ultimate goal of the Performance Matrix: it helps a player determine not only where they are, but ultimately where they want to go during their playing career. I remind my players often of the famous quote, it is not where you start but where you finish that matters.

This particular point is worth repeating. Irrespective of the statistics, I believe every player should work to become the best athletic version of themselves possible. This is how a player can succeed during their competitive playing career and eliminates one of life's frustrations: regret.

Competitor (Low/Average Skill, High Effort Player)

Competitive players inspire me as a coach. They bring their absolute best effort and a can-attitude to every task, irrespective of their starting skill or talent levels. As a result, they truly become the best sports version of themselves possible and help their team become successful.[13]

As a coach, this is the quadrant you want every one of your players to be in. You want them to be competitors and live at the high end of the effort spectrum. A person's best effort, after all, is the prerequisite to learning, development, and growth in sports and life. If you want to become your personal best, you have to bring your personal best effort.

I love the Gutt Check Performance Matrix and make sure to discuss the model at every player and parent preseason meeting, and even include a short description of it in our team's playbook. I use the Gutt Check Matrix so often that by the time a player reaches their senior season they know it so well they can flawlessly explain it to the freshman. The Seniors even put together a little ad-hoc spoof to tease me about it before one game too, it was hilarious!

I leverage the Performance Matrix during games too. For example, during a game a few years ago the players and team were not performing up to their full potential. At intermission I simply drew the matrix on the locker room whiteboard for a little team gut check.

> "Where are you right now, where are we right now as a team? We live here." *(I circled and pointed to the matrix "compete" category.)* "Now get out there and outwork your opponents; compete!"

I also use the Gutt Check Performance Matrix when needed during player (and player-parent) feedback sessions. I start the discussion by asking, "Where do you feel

MANAGE EXPECTATIONS

you are on my matrix during games and practices right now?" This question starts the discussion and reminds the players, and their parents, that in sports and life, you get what you earn, through hard work.

My mom left our earthly bounds long ago, but I'm pretty confident she knew exactly what she was doing when she hand-painted those ceramic mugs. It was her way of sending a simple message: if you are going to play, play your best. After nearly three decades of searching, I found a similarly simple way of setting and managing expectations for my players and parents.

The Gutt Check Performance Matrix simplifies the learning process by leveraging the two factors that drive all others, effort and skill. This is how you can easily set and manage expectations for your young players and their parents.

I am so confident about the relationships the cycle and matrix bring to bear, that if you were to ask me for a singular recommendation or sound-bite, I'd say use the Gutt Check Performance Matrix, it works! The Performance Matrix is the easiest way I have found to set and manage expectations for players and parents. I'm confident its simplicity would make my mom proud.

HUSTLE AND HAVE FUN!

Endnotes

10 The cycle of continuous improvement through sports contains 5-element's: effort, skills improvement, belief, competition, and grit. This is a process I've named the *Gutt Check Improvement Cycle*. Development of this cycle was instrumental in establishing the cause-effect relationships required to develop the Gutt Check Performance Matrix. The cycle defines the culture of effective teams, effective coaches, and successful people.

11 Definition of gut-check as it appears in Oxford Languages and Google online dictionary. A "Gutt Check" is my way of using a gut check assessment to determine the actions required to accomplish meaningful duties.

12 The 10,000-hour rule was coined by Malcolm Gladwell. Gladwell contends it takes that many personal practice hours to develop elite-level skills, whether that is sports, acting, or playing an instrument. See *Outliers: The*

Story of Success, by Malcolm Gladwell. This book is cited in the appendix.

13 Coach Pete Carrol focuses on the importance of competition in his book *Win Forever: Live, Work, and Play Like a Champion*. See the appendix for the full citation.

Fourth: Act Like the Role Model You Are

Become the best coaching version of you possible

In my early twenties I won my first head coaching job for an under eleven-year-old team in North Dakota. I excitedly entered the locker room for my first practice with the team and heard the crunch of small pieces of white glass under my boots. An unknown "someone" had broken every light bulb in the room with a hockey stick, except for one of course, so the others had enough light to witness the stupidity.

After all the players were on the ice for practice, I told them to line up on the side boards. Then I blew the whistle for over and backs. No words or "Hi, I'm the new coach" speech. I simply defaulted to the coaching behavior I had witnessed when I was a player growing up and we misbehaved: disciplinary coaching using conditioning as punishment. Unfortunately, this style of coaching worked. We ended the season by finishing third at our level in the state that year.

The next season my military service brought me to Ohio and a voluntary coaching job for an under fourteen-year-old hockey team. I defaulted to the disciplinarian style of coaching with this team too, after all, it worked in North Dakota.

HUSTLE AND HAVE FUN!

Early in the season my team had an away game against a tough opponent. For the first twelve minutes of the game, my team was locked in the defensive end of the ice. I was furious the other team's players were peppering our goalie mercilessly, while my players seemingly sat and watched.

It's embarrassing to recall and write about, to be honest, but during the first intermission, I let my emotions take full control of my behavior. I started yelling and screaming at the players and stopped teaching and coaching.

> "You're letting them skate around you like you are traffic cones! Nobody is taking the body, nobody is clearing rebounds. You're playing like a bunch of five-year-olds! Would you let someone push you around like that in the school hallway? Toughen up!!"

For at least a minute I went on, getting louder and more uncontrollably colorful as I went. I acted like this, by the way, in a 1950s-era ice rink where the fan seating was right behind the players' bench. The parents were so close to my tirade, I could have leaned over for a handful of their popcorn.

The next period started, and we played even worse. After the game, I got in my truck and began the always-longer-after-a-loss drive home. I was upset, not at the players or the game result, but at myself. I was embarrassed by my behavior.

Over the next self-reflective week or two, I came to realize I was impersonating a blend of the coaches I had grown up playing for as a youth player myself. I was mirroring how they would have reacted if the teams I played on were losing, one-step behind, and continually out of position. I was mimicking and parroting them instead of learning to become the best version of myself as a coach. I was simply not being authentic.

Coaches you grew up playing for, watched on television, or read about may provide you with examples to learn from, but you should avoid mimicking them. Your players will be able to tell when you are being authentic and sincere as their coach or when you are *acting* like a coach. This Dr. Jekyll and Mr. Hyde kind of coaching only confuses the players making you less effective as their teacher and leader.

I eventually came to realize there were stark differences between the teams I grew up playing for, and the Ohio teenagers I was coaching decades later. For instance, as a player myself I had more practice time in two days than the Ohioans had in a week. I also had free outdoor ice to utilize for informal practices, whereas the Southwest Ohio players did not. I could not coach the Ohio team like they were my late-1970s team, because they were not equivalent. The team I was coaching was distinctly different and my disciplinary coaching style was extremely unproductive.

My Ohio hockey players did not lose the game because they didn't care, or didn't try. We lost the game because we simply did not have the skill, speed, or stamina of our Northern Ohio opponents. No amount of screaming or yelling was going to change that simple fact. I learned that **to be an effective coach, you have to focus on the team you have, not the team you wish you had**. But I was too young, inexperienced, and immature as a coach to understand the difference up until that point in time. As a result of my ignorance, instead of learning something of value in the loss, my Ohio hockey players only learned that their coach was a hot-head.

The season with my Ohio teenagers taught me a corollary lesson as well, something I learned playing little-league baseball but had forgotten somewhere along the line. **To be an effective coach you must control your emotions, and cannot let your emotions control you.** This does not mean you can't get upset or angry at times. After all you are human, and there is no doubt enthusiastic emotion (even yelling) may be required at times to address an issue or concern. A missed call by a referee that endangers a player needs to be addressed. An athlete not giving their best effort, missing assignments, or being a negative influence needs to be addressed as well. A coach must "get them moving" at times. I get it. But you have to use your emotions consciously, in a manner you can live with, justify, and maybe even smile about afterward.

An effective coach uses their emotions consciously for positive effect, not as a way to punish a player or relieve their personal stresses. A good coach remains calm, controlled, humble, and empathetic even during the heat of battle.

Whenever I see a coach losing their composure, I wonder why they feel validated by winning, and invalidated by losing. Coaching is not about your personal need for affirmation, it's about teaching the players' life skills. Quid-pro-quo type of coaching is not effective long-term, the players do not learn valuable life-lessons from inflammatory outbursts. **The validation you should be seeking as a coach is when a player (or the players) learns something of value from every contest: win, lose, or tie.** This type of coaching helps players become self-motivated, self-sufficient human beings. This will not happen if the only time a

ACT LIKE THE ROLE MODEL YOU ARE

player gets moving is when an adult is telling them, or worse, yelling them to.

Famous athletes, presidents, physicians, Nobel prize winners, and more are often asked "Who was the person that positively influenced you the most growing up?" More times than not, they answer by telling us about their favorite teacher or coach. That is how influential you are as a secondary role model, whether you realize it or not.

You should want to be remembered as a coach who pushed, challenged, mentored, and motivated your players. The coach who believed in them and helped them believe in themselves. The coach who cared about them and their personal success. The coach who suffered no foolishness and held them personally accountable for their actions, on and off the playing field. This type of emotionally mature coach is the kind of secondary adult role model your young and impressionable players deserve.[14]

Endnotes

14 This is known as emotional maturity or emotional intelligence. For more on this topic, see *Primal Leadership, Learning to Lead with Emotional Intelligence*. Full citation appears in the appendix.

Fifth: Treat the Parents Like Adults

Even if they are acting like children

Let's discuss the elephant in the room. I know some coaches and referees have commented the players' parents are driving them out of their respective sports. I have heard other coaches say the parents are making it too hard, or coaching is not fun anymore because of them. I'm highly confident friends of yours have already warned you about "the parents" as well. This is a sad testament to sports in total.

I am the parent of players myself, and I've seen the referees who let games get too physical or out of control. I've witnessed the basketball coach who hasn't put a player into the game despite the fact the team was winning by over thirty points, and only three minutes remained on the clock. Frustrating; I know.

But nothing truly justifies a grown man yelling obscenities at the teenage referee at a soccer game between eight-year-olds. Or the police being called after parents of ten-year-old hockey players engage in a brawl in the parking lot after a game. Who are the children when this type of behavior is going on? As I remind my own kids, age and maturity are not always correlated.

Only a very small minority of my parental interactions have driven my wife and me to ask the question: why am I still doing this? Fortunately, most of the parents I have interacted with as a coach have been an absolute pleasure to work with. This positive perspective is the one I recommend you take as a coach because working with, not against, the parents is absolutely essential. **The parents are key stakeholders in the sport, and the players will learn more when everyone works together: coach, player, and parent.**

In any working relationship there should be healthy boundaries. I have tried several sets of "parent rules" over the years aimed at calming down my emotions, and those of the parents, so a conversation between mature adults could ensue. However, despite my best intentions there are those obscure situations the rules do not accommodate, or the parent who doesn't give a crap about them.

Before jumping into my parental rule set, I want to share a little trick I learned along the way to help keep my emotions under control. My technique is best told using a story from my childhood.

My brothers and I were Dad's snowplow and had the chore of manually shoveling snow off the family driveway each winter. After a healthy snowfall, and once the chore was complete, it was time for some fun!

The four of us would pair up two-to-a-side of the driveway, and tuck behind the two large piles of snow that always accumulated near the road on both sides of the drive. The teams had a few minutes to prepare their snowball weapons, and while doing so I'd whisper a strategy to my brotherly teammate. "You throw one high in the air, and while they are watching that one, I'll throw a fastball right at them."

Once the snow weapons were ready, it was "3-2-1" and go! Just like we planned, my brother-teammate lobbed a high arching aerial bomb, and our blood-line opponents took the bait by looking skyward. At that exact moment, I moved to the side of my snow mountain and launched a line-drive direct-fire hit to an opponent's chest. The strategy worked every time!

After telling this story to various audiences over the years, I'd swing my arm in a high arc over my head, pause, and say "interesting." Then I'd make a baseball pitcher's motion for a fastball straight in, pause, and say "relevant."

Fully grasping the difference between interesting and relevant is a skill everyone in today's society needs, especially your players. They are bombarded 24/7/365 with so-called "information" on social media. Unfortunately, your players are mostly exposed to stupidity traveling at the speed of light. This is why teaching them to differentiate between interesting or relevant, fact or fiction, and even truth or lies is so critical. The ability to distinguish between these two terms is a key life skill like all others.

The parent yelling at you about their child's playing time is interesting. Their child being taught to bring their best effort in all they do is relevant. A parent complaining about their player being called out for extra conditioning is interesting. The player learning they are personally responsible and accountable for their behavior is relevant. You get the point.

Separating interesting from relevant is an easy way to help keep your emotions in check even when a parent is being overly emotional and calling you an idiot or worse. This leads me to a prerequisite rule when dealing with a player's parent(s).

Never hold the player accountable for their parent's misbehavior.

Protecting the players' growth and development is relevant, their parents' misbehavior is interesting. An effective coach never punishes a player for the parent's misdeeds. Doing so would be unfair to the player, and only teach them not to trust you or any other adult authority figure.

Whether the parents' criticism is fair or unfair, emotional or not, you have to remain calm, unemotional, and mature. As I was told many years ago, there is a kernel of truth in all criticism. Effective coaches seek to understand the parents' main point and take it as a learning opportunity. This is how you can receive feedback, even brutally honest or unfairly negative criticism, the right way. **An effective coach acts like an adult, and treats the parents the same, even if a parent is acting childish.**

The goal of parental interaction and communication is to keep the conversation relevant, player-centric, and unemotional. The gold standard to get to this utopian environment is the "24-hour no-contact" rule. It simply does not work. Overly emotional parents do not give a flying puck about your 24-hour rule. When the game ends, they will make a bee-line right to you, even entering the locker room to do so. The bottom line is the situation the 24-hour rule is intended to avoid, it doesn't, which is why I stopped using it altogether.

Instead, I recommend coaches adopt the following three alternative rules which I have found enhance communication with a coach's number one stakeholders: the parents. There's a complementary fourth rule for the parent coach below as well.

TREAT THE PARENTS LIKE ADULTS

1. I'll talk to any parent, about any subject, at any time. But the request to do so must come from your student-athlete.

Many times, when I was talking with a parent about their player, it would become crystal clear the parent was expressing their own frustrations, not those of their player. To confirm my hunch, I'd seek some feedback directly from the student-athlete. What I would learn is the player "got it," and fully understood the best effort team philosophy, and the consequences of not bringing it (missing a shift, less playing time). The players got it, but their parents did not. You must remember that the players are young and most likely do not properly communicate with their parents about the coach's feedback. As a result, Mom and Dad are left in the dark where the seeds of frustration can grow. This is why I make sure to share a subordinate rule with the players and parents every season.

You, as the parent, cannot care more about it than your player does.

Trust me, I have to remind my wife and myself about this principle frequently during our children's sports seasons. After a game where my daughter didn't get a lot of playing time, her attitude was "Oh well." My wife and I were upset she didn't play and asked her "What did you do to deserve this?" By the way, this is not a good way to start a discussion, unless it's an inquisition. Our daughter just shrugged her shoulders and asked "What's for dinner?"

Mom and Dad should not care more about the sport than their child does, it is just not logical. The parents' feelings are interesting while the players' thoughts are relevant.

This simple rule and subordinate principle forces the parent and player to have a conversation and get on the same page, prior to engaging with the coach. It works.

2. You can say anything you want to about a player, as long as it is positive and that player shares your last name.

I grew up playing three sports through high school and have coached for decades. I thought I had seen it all until my youngest daughter started playing basketball. I actually witnessed a parent from the opposing team use hand gestures toward her daughter on the court, indicating she would give her daughter twenty dollars for "taking out" a certain player on my daughter's team. Yes, this is a true story, and it happened at an eight-year-old girls' basketball game!

Overly emotional parents significantly decrease their player's "fun" factor, which is why I was not surprised to learn years later that the player in this story no longer plays basketball.

The "share your last name" rule keeps the parent focused on their child and the effort that player is bringing to bear, rather than blaming other players for their child's underperformance (e.g. Mike never passes to my kid). This rule helps me remind the parents the player owns one hundred percent of the effort and attitude they bring to the sport, nobody else.

I like to use the mirror to make this particular point to players who start the blame game.

"You keep looking in the mirror and seeing others: your parents, teammates, and coaches. You are blaming them instead of seeing the only reflection that truly matters: yours. You control your own effort and attitude, no one else."

If all youth coaches adopted this rule, and all sports parents followed it, we would have a very positive athletic experience for our impressionable youth players.

3. It is not about "like," it is about effort.

I'll be honest, I cannot stand to hear "coach doesn't like me" from my children. It's never about like, I remind them, it's always about effort. A coach wants the same thing from every player; for the player to bring their best effort, support their teammates, and help the team be successful.

When a player is not getting into a game at a competitive youth or high school level, it's not because the coach does not like the player. It is more likely because the player has failed to learn from mistakes and is repeating them, blaming others, or generally being a negative influence on the team. It is not personal. It is a coach letting a player know, you didn't help your team very well right there, so sit down and think about how you can be a better teammate next time. It's an effectual coach holding a player personally responsible and accountable for their actions, or inactions. It's good coaching.

I make sure to conduct a pre-season player and parent meeting every year. The main thing I cover during this meeting is the Gutt Check Performance Matrix from the previous chapter. I have found the matrix helps the parents understand our team's "best-effort" philosophy. My request to the parents during the meeting is if they hear their player ever say, "Coach doesn't like me," to respond as I would by asking them "Where do you believe you are on the Coach's Matrix right now?" It's never about like, it's always about effort.

There is one final rule I recommend for the coach who has a son or daughter on their team. This rule will help you avoid the mistake I made early on coaching my son and daughters' teams: tunnel-vision. I tended to see the ice rink or field full of players through a soda straw focused on one player, my child.

I first recognized this channelized-attention phenomena between an assistant coach and his player son. As soon as the player finished a shift and returned to the bench for a respite, they immediately looked to their parent coach for validation. If the parent coach did not provide immediate positive affirmations, their child's head sunk to the floor.

After seeing this interaction, I started to police my own behavior. I was guilty of the same thing, and I later learned it was negatively affecting my son's "fun factor" too! Which led to the following rule for the parent-coach.

4. As a parent coach, do not coach your child during practices or games, coach the team instead.

As the parent coach, if you want something emphasized or corrected in your son's or daughter's play, ask another coach to do it. For example, during games or practices, when I noticed something my son had done wrong, I would look at an assistant coach, and say, "did you see that?" The assistant would smile and say, "Yeah, I got it," and as soon as my son got off the ice to rest, the assistant did the job of teaching. The other parent-coaches on the team did the same.

This rule enhanced both player and parent-coaches overall enjoyment of the sport and allowed me, and the other parent coaches, to focus on the entire team of players, not just one. To make sure this rule was fully understood and followed, I also added a corollary rule during games and practices for the *player* whose mom or dad is coaching them.

There's no Mom or Dad here, only your coach.

I believe it is important for your child to view you as a coach to keep everyone in the right frame of mind during games and practices. It also reminds the other players "coach's kid" is not going to get special treatment; they have to earn it too. Trust me, at first it will feel strangely correct to hear "Coach" and not "Mom or Dad" from your child when you are their coach.

This subordinate rule helps your child recognize you are working hard to do what is right for all the players, not just one.

The goal of parental interaction and communication is to keep the conversation relevant, player-centric, and unemotional. I am confident these simple rules will help you become an effective communicator with your number one stakeholder: the parents.

So far, we have covered the top-level coaching recommendations I have for youth coaches. Next, I want to turn your attention to the more tactical day-to-day recommendations you can leverage to be a more effective teacher of sport.

Sixth: Run Balanced Practices

Practice skills development, team play, and conditioning to bring out your players' personal best

In the 2016 to 2017 season I was hired to coach my local high school hockey team. We had a few practices as a team and then headed up north for a pre-season warm-up contest. The team started strong and had earned a 4 to 0 lead after two periods of play against a well-oiled Toledo Ohio-based team. Then the wheels fell off the bus and in the final fifteen minutes of play, our opponents scored five goals. Yes, five! We lost a four-goal lead in the final period of play, which is something professional coaches get fired over. Good thing I was not a professional coach!

If you were at this game, you would have been mortified or laughing. It was a sight to behold: players banging their sticks on the ice, blaming each other, not believing in their teammates, and failing to put in the effort required to be successful. One of the players even muttered under their breath, "we're not a third period team." I let loose after the game.

> "We're not a third period team? Really? No! We are out of shape, and we spend invaluable time banging our sticks on the ice in frustration rather than quickly recovering from the mistake and hustling back to protect your goalie!"

I came away from the game concluding the players were out of shape, and it was my job to fix it. The problem was in doing so, it was perceived by the players and assistants the extra conditioning was punishment for blowing a four-goal lead and losing a game.

After one practice consisting of numerous conditioning-based drills, an assistant coach asked to talk to me. "You know Greg, conditioning shouldn't be punishment," he said. "You have to get the players to see it as a positive, as a necessary part of the game."

This great assistant coach was one hundred percent correct. **An effective coach recognizes conditioning is a vital part of the game and incorporates it into every practice in some manner.** Over and backs, board-to-boards, or shuttle runs in practice build muscle mass in your players' legs and core. It strengthens a player's quadriceps and hamstrings; the key leg muscles for power, speed, and stamina in sports like hockey.

Conditioning also enhances a player's mental toughness. Thinking "I'm exhausted," "I'm too tired," "We can't win anyway," or "What's the point" are reasons a player gives up on themselves and their teammates. When you let self-doubt creep in you give rise to the thoughts of quitting. As I said earlier, an important aspect of coaching is moving a player from *I can't* to *I can*, and conditioning is an important element to instill a sense of self-belief and grit into a player's psyche.

I worked over time to change the players viewpoint on conditioning, and eventually they embraced it as a necessary tool to enhance our game-day performance. Nonetheless, games still slipped out of reach in the final fifteen

RUN BALANCED PRACTICES

minutes of play throughout the entire season.

During the following spring and summer, I replayed the losses in my mind and realized conditioning was not the problem we were having in the final period of each game. The players were in great shape and battled to the bitter end of every game that season but just could not tip the scale their way. I eventually came to understand the problem was not the players, it was their coach.

My team of eleven skaters and two goalies routinely played against teams with eighteen skaters and two goalies. We were outnumbered in almost every game, yet I was implementing a team play equivalent to a full-court press in basketball.[15] I foolishly had the team pressing all game long with drastically fewer players than our opponents. My players were outnumbered and the team play I was implementing brought them to the edge of exhaustion.

What I learned through this experience is **an effective coach sets and practices team plays that match the skill and stamina levels of the team.** This leads me to the second element necessary to run balanced practices: properly exercising the team plays your team will need to execute on game-day(s).

The next season I implemented a more conservative "zone" style offensive attack which better matched our roster size and capabilities. The result of this change has not only helped the team compete for the entirety of a full forty-five-minute game, it has carried us to the top of the league standings for four consecutive seasons.

It is worth noting a related lesson I learned along the way. That is, **an effective coach assigns players to the positions best suited for their particular individual skill and capability levels too**. Six seasons ago I moved a lifelong forward to defense. I felt the player would see the ice better from that position, and become a more explosive playmaker and offensive threat. It was a tough transition, but he embraced it and graduated from high school as the top defensive record-holder by every measure: goals, assists, points, and plus-minus.[16]

Regardless of your team's plays, if the players can't skate, shoot, pass, or stickhandle, they won't be able to execute them. This is why **the third and final element required to include in your balanced practice plan is focused skills development.**

When I was around eleven years old my hockey coach noticed I favored crossing my right leg in front of my left, for a counter-clockwise tight skating turn. "Gutt," the coach said during a practice, "You'll skate halfway around the world to get to the right-side boards so you can cut hard from right to left behind their defensemen." He then said, "I want you to get on the center circle and do clockwise cross-overs (right turns) until I tell you to stop." While the rest of the team warmed up for practice, I was doing clockwise right-turns on the center circle by myself. My player-centric coach had me do this focused skills-development activity at the beginning of practices for weeks, until I finally mastered the skill.

Without the ability to effectively turn both ways while skating, I never would have landed at the NCAA Division I level of the sport. My youth coach recognized how important skills development was to helping this particular player reach his full potential. This is exactly what effective coaches do, they set an enabling environment so their players can reach their full potential.

Anyone who has ever watched youth basketball has seen

RUN BALANCED PRACTICES

the impact of limited skills development. Every game, coach-after-coach, verbally direct their players defensively by repeating the phrase, "get her on her left hand." It seems obvious if you want to take away a defensive play from your opponent's basketball playbook, you should teach all the players on your team to dribble the ball with their left (or non-dominant) hand. But if that was the case, I wouldn't have this example to share. The point is **limited skills development limits players and stifles teams.**

Well-balanced practice plans include three key elements required to empower your players to become their very best: conditioning, team play, and skills development. The more innovative you are designing practice drills to combine the elements of a balanced practice, the more effective and efficient your practices will be. More importantly, the players will learn, grow, and develop faster too.

Before I leave this topic there are three additional recommendations I'd like to pass along to help you run awesome practices. First, as I'm sure you know, repetition is the key to skills development and muscle memory. Design your practice plan to maximize repetitions and keep the players moving. One way to do this is to employ station or circuit-based drills during practices.

For example, I like to take the first fifteen minutes of an hour-long practice and work on three specific hockey skills (e.g. skating, shooting, passing). I do this by breaking the ice into three sections, stations, or circuits.[17] Each station has an assigned coach and skill drill to execute. I then break up the team into three small groups and assign each group to a station. I blow the whistle to start the 5-minute session, and then blow the whistle again and yell "rotate" after five-minutes have transpired. The players move to a new station where they begin working on a different focused skill.

I do this one more time to complete the cycle, so in the short span of fifteen minutes the players have worked on three specific and different skills. The small group sizes ensure each player accomplishes numerous repetitions of the skill, and by doing so, they begin developing the muscle memory required to add the skill to their repertoire. Plus, by keeping players in constant motion, you up the fun ante in practices.

You can accomplish this practice process as a solo coach too. Just set up the stations and demonstrate the skills for the players before dividing them into small groups. Make sure to identify a lead for each group who can help to keep things moving at the unsupervised station, and then send the groups to their initial stations. While the team is actively engaged in focused skills development, you can move from station-to-station correcting form and function while motivating the players to do their best.

Secondly, when you are developing a practice plan make sure to build skills and team plays incrementally. It's the "crawl, walk, run" learning model. For example, before you teach the team an effective *three-versus-two* offensive rush, teach the players how to execute a *two-versus-zero*, then a *two-versus-one, two-versus-two,* and ultimately a *three-versus-two*.

I strongly recommend you do not advance to the next iteration of the team play until players can consistently perform the easier play. By progressively building the team-play, block-by-block, the players have the foundation to run the play(s) regardless of where they find themselves on the ice during contests. They will also know what they should do whether they are the quarterback in possession of the puck or not. This is how your players will learn to read, react, and innovate.

My final tactical recommendation for executing effective and efficient practices is to combine conditioning, team-play, and/or skills development into a single drill whenever possible. For example, during a two-on-zero offensive rush drill, adding another player who is chasing her teammates from behind, makes the activity a game-like team play requiring passing and skating skills, as well as a conditioning drill. The game-like realism embeds the physical and mental muscle memory players need to compete at their very best levels too, especially when they are tired.[18]

The bottom line is that to bring out the players' best efforts, build their self-confidence, and provide some challenges they need to overcome, you should run effective and efficient practices. Including conditioning, team play, and skills-development in practices is the best way to set the conditions for growth, development, and learning for both the players and the team.

Endnotes

15 I was using a 2-1-2 forecheck where two offensive players pursue the puck in the offensive end of the ice aggressively. This is similar to a full court press in basketball.

16 Plus-minus is a hockey statistic. All the players on the ice receive a plus (+) when a goal is scored for their team. All players on the ice receive a minus (-) when they are on the ice and the opponent scores a goal.

17 USA Hockey's American Development Model (ADM) emphasizes skill-station focused practices, and has printable practice plans available for all age groups available at *USAhockey.com*. This is a great resource I highly recommend you utilize. The skills drills are easily modified for use by other team sports coaches too.

18 "Hard training builds mental and physical "muscle memory" that pays dividends when exhaustion sets in." This is an interpretation of World War II General George Patton's quote: "an ounce of sweat, will save a gallon of blood." See bibliography for full citation.

Seventh: Treat Games as Your Primary Classroom

Players are more receptive to learning before, during, and after games

A few seasons ago my high school team was scheduled to play an early morning holiday tournament game. The fact the game was at 7:30 in the morning was bad; the fact it was against a top ten team in Ohio made it cruel and inhumane.

Before what was expected-to-be a lopsided game began, I followed our normal pre-game team ritual. I wrote out the keys to the game on my portable whiteboard: communication, positioning, and have fun!

I have found this simple method helps the players get in the right game mindset while they are putting on their equipment. (By the way, another good practice to eliminate distractions and keep your players in game mode is to have them put away their phones.)

In addition to writing down the keys to the game, I like to discuss our game strategy before they stretch, and give a pep talk before we depart the locker room for the game. These are important talks in my book. You can't get on a player during a game for not implementing a plan you did not cover thoroughly during your pre-game strategy talk. And although a coach is not one hundred percent responsible for the emotion and energy a player brings to the contest, your impact on their emotional readiness should not be underestimated.

HUSTLE AND HAVE FUN!

Despite the opponent, I always make sure there is a key lesson the players take away from every game; something they take with them to make them better players, a better team, and stronger people down the road.[19] This was the focus of my pre-game strategy talk to the team that early Saturday morning.

> "We are playing against a top ten team in the state. You are all mature players; you've seen the stats. We may be outgunned this morning. That doesn't mean we quit or give up. We fight, we work. As a result, we will learn something new that will make us better players and a better team down the road.
>
> Let's make sure to focus on what we can control. We can control our effort and attitude. We can control our positioning. And we can clear rebounds. These are the simple things we can do to improve.
>
> I have seen too many of you panicking with the puck in the defensive zone this season. So today, your job is to get the puck on your stick, be poised, shoot it high off the glass, and clear the puck out of our zone. If that results in an icing call, that is absolutely ok.[20] We will learn to be poised with the puck, and how to properly ice it. That is a skill and team play we will need down the line, so let's work on that this morning."

I returned to the locker room for the pre-game pep talk after the players were stretched, dressed, and ready to play.

> "I'll keep this one short and sweet. You control your effort and attitude. Go out there and be proud of your effort. Don't worry about the scoreboard, only your effort. Stay positive with one another. And today,

TREAT GAMES AS YOUR PRIMARY CLASSROOM

when you have the puck on your stick near our goalie, take possession, have some poise, and clear it out of our zone and down the ice. Alright, let's go have some fun!"

"Have fun" is always one of the game themes I write down on the whiteboard. This is a game after all, and although it is taken seriously at times, players should have fun learning and competing. The "Two H's," hustle and have fun, are my coaching cornerstones.

The game started and as expected, our faster, stronger, more skilled opponents controlled the pace and play. The puck was in our end of the rink, the defensive zone, almost the entire first period.

I kept reinforcing, "poise, possession, ice the puck" and eventually our team actually started to follow the gameplan. The other team quickly became frustrated by our delay tactic, and instead of working together for possession in a game of keep-away, they defaulted to individualism. Our players maintained disciplined positioning, and eventually, the opponents' selfish play resulted in a mistake.

Late in the first period of play, our player grabbed a loose puck near our goalie and sent it high into the air near the defensive zone's blue line. One of our opponents' defensemen went to catch the puck as a baseball player would, but it deflected off his hockey glove instead and landed in the middle of the ice rink. One of our players took advantage and skated past their defenseman to win the loose puck, and earned a break-away one-on-one with the opponent's goalie. Our player's shot was perfectly placed, and it hit the netting behind the goalie for a goal. This was literally our only shot on the other team's goalie during the first period, and miraculously we were winning the game 1 to 0.

Midway through the second period of play another opponent defenseman made the exact same error, and we capitalized again. We now had two shots on their goal and were winning the game 2 to 0 despite the fact our opponent's possessed the puck ninety-seven percent of the time and had generated north of thirty shots on our goalie. While I watched the other team's coaches losing their minds yelling at their players, I could not stop smiling in disbelief.

The relentless attack by our opponents eventually wore every player on my roster down, and the game ended as a lopsided 2 to 10 loss. But our team was successful that day nonetheless. They took a game-plan to "learn something new" and brilliantly executed it. Even in a loss, there must be learning. Even in a loss, there can be a success.

I'll cover the importance of the post-game talk to conclude this chapter. But before I do, let's discuss four things you can do to properly manage the bench during a game.

First, your players will be watching you very closely before, during, and after a game. If you are nervous, they will be. If you are cavalier, they will be too. If you lose your mind, they will follow suit. But if you remain calm, they will remain calm.

We have all seen the impact on the players from a coach who loses control of their emotions. Their players get angry, overly aggressive, unsafe, start fights, and yell obscenities at everyone, including the referees and even the parents in the stands. Never forget you are an important secondary role model and you set the example for the players to emulate. If you want a first-class team, you have to be a first-class coach by setting the tone and environment correctly for your players.

Second, the players in the game cannot understand a

TREAT GAMES AS YOUR PRIMARY CLASSROOM

single word you are saying. They may hear it, but they won't be able to process it and perform at their peak levels at the same time. The only thing they likely hear from a boisterous coach on the sidelines is the "blah, blah, blah" of Charlie Brown's teacher.

The effective coach focuses their comments and editorials on the players on the bench, using the players in the game as their real-time examples. This type of coach also realizes the players not in possession of the puck (or ball), are the best examples to use while doing so.

Statistics show that ninety-eight percent of the time a player is engaged in a game, they are doing so without possession of the puck.[21] This is likely where the paradigm "What you do without the ball is just as important as what you do with it" originated.

Here are a few examples of this principle to consider, and remember, they are directed toward the players on the bench, using the players in the game not in possession of the puck as examples.

> Brian is doing great! He's forcing them to the boards with perfect strong-side backchecking.
>
> Look at Mike, do you see he is in perfect defensive position down low by the goalie?
>
> Perfect positioning by Tony, see how he is taking away the skating, shooting, and passing lanes defensively?
>
> John's doing a great job getting open by creating time and space for himself.

Focusing your comments toward the players on the bench, and reinforcing the positive play of their teammates without the puck (or ball) in the game, underscores your expectations of them when they are in the game.

Unfortunately, this is sometimes easier said than done. I have no doubt, if you were to ask my players, I'm sure you'll hear I'm guilty of focusing on the negatives instead of reinforcing the positives at times. Nevertheless, to hold yourself and your assistants to this standard, remind them (and yourself) often to focus their comments toward the players on bench, not on the ice.

The final two recommendations for effective game management are best summarized by a short recap of a game I coached not too long ago. This particular story will highlight the two game-management recommendations above as well.

My high school team earned their way into the semi-final game of our league playoffs and was set to play a very good team from Southwest Ohio. To set the stage a little, we had two seniors on our roster compared to our opponents' ten. If you haven't seen how seniors play in what may be their final career game, it's something to behold. Everything is left on the ice; especially in this game, because it was a home game for our opponents.

Within the first seven minutes of play, before some of the parents could even sit down with their snacks, we found ourselves behind by three goals. Our players were frustrated, upset, and frankly a little shocked. I was too! I started to really watch the action on the ice so I could figure out what the other team was doing to put us on our heels. As I was silently reflecting on our dilemma, I heard a few of the players start playing the blame game. They were debating who had made the mistake that led to the third goal against us.

My third recommendation for effective game management is to **pay attention to how the players are communicating with each other, and ensures it remains constructive, not destructive.** It is perfectly acceptable for players to hold each other accountable; this is a team sport after all. But it is important for any type of communication between the players to never cross the line from demanding, to demeaning.

"Listen, and look at me," I said to them twice before they realized I was serious and turned my way. "I have never seen a team be successful by blaming each other. Never! Now stop worrying about each other, stop worrying about the scoreboard, and start worrying about outworking your opponents on both ends of the ice!"

During games like these, and there will be a lot of them, you have to keep your composure. Yelling at the players, being negative, or giving up is not teaching them anything of value. As we discussed earlier, you are a secondary adult role model, and as such you should model the type of behavior you would want to see from the players when they are adults in tough conversations or situations.

In my three decades of coaching youth sports, I have seen my fair share of these types of games. I have learned when you have that "what the heck is going on" feeling, your first and only focus should be to make sure your players continue to give their very best effort. I do this by repeating phrases like, "The scoreboard is interesting; your effort is relevant. Get moving. Outwork them!"

Once your players are working hard, then you have to identify the source of the bleeding and make adjustments.

Doing nothing will not inspire confidence in you as their coach, and even if your team play tuning makes it worse, the changes bring about learning, for you and your players.

Making the real-time adjustments needed to give your players a chance to be more competitive is my fourth and final recommendation for effective game management.

My triaging technique is to start watching the ongoing game as if it was on television. This helps me momentarily remove myself from the game emotionally, so I can begin to critically think about where the damage is coming from. I go silent during this process so I can remove as many distractions as possible from my mind. Many coaches will use the intermissions or half-time to make team play adjustments. But I have learned when you are getting shellacked early, you need to make adjustments early.

Once you have identified the source of the pain, I recommend you make small and simple adjustments. It is too hard to make major adjustments during a game, and it will only confuse and frustrate your players. The minor corrective actions help your players see you are in control, not because you are screaming and yelling, but because you are thinking and tweaking your game-plan.

I went into "watching" mode during this game and I identified the problem. Our opponent was overloading the weak side of the ice near our goalie. Their opportunities resulted from the fact they were outnumbering us in this critical piece of real estate.

I called for the players on the bench's attention and said, "Listen, we need our winger to get low by the net to help the defenseman cover the weak side.[22] This will leave their defenseman open by the blue line, but that is okay. The

TREAT GAMES AS YOUR PRIMARY CLASSROOM

wing can still get in the lane and block the shot if the puck gets out to their Defenseman." I reinforced this principle again during the first intermission.

In the second period the ice leveled and play was fast and physical on both ends of the rink. Just before the end of the second period, though, a great play and perfect snipe (shot) resulted in a goal for the good guys. We entered the second intermission down 1 goal to 3.

Believing in yourself, your teammates, and your game plan is a powerful emotional motivator. During the second intermission, we talked about the changes we made to our formations and how they were working.

> "You have turned the tide with some great goaltending, defense, and shooting. As a result, they are getting nervous. You are in better shape and you are wearing them down. Remember our forecheck, it is a way to conserve energy and make them burn more. Use it. They are getting tired and will take dumb penalties as a result. When they do, make it count and score on the power-play. Don't worry about the scoreboard, just worry about outworking them. Let's go win the third period!"

You guessed it. We scored two goals in the third period and took the game into overtime. Behind some stellar goaltending, one of our players eventually earned a goal to win the game and put us into the league's championship game for the fourth year in a row. **Gritty, never-quit, team-oriented cultures matter, in sports and life**.

You may have noticed my intermission speech reinforced the importance of working hard in practices. Statements like "You are in better shape," reinforces the positive impact of conditioning. "Remember our forecheck,"

HUSTLE AND HAVE FUN!

reinforces the team play and how important it is to our overall game-day success. And recognizing "great goaltending, defense, and shooting" provides positive reinforcement of why a player's hard work on and off ice to develop their skills is essential.

The post-game talk is the most important teaching opportunity you will have as a coach because you have two critical elements required for true learning. First, games stir up significant emotions, and second, you momentarily have the players' undivided attention. I have learned you have less than ninety seconds to make your teaching points before the players begin daydreaming. For maximum effect keep your comments short, sweet, and focused on the character traits that will sustain the players throughout their lives.

I mentioned earlier in this chapter an early morning game against a top ten team resulted in a 2 to 10 drubbing. After that game I went into the locker room to teach.

> "Before the game, we talked about learning something new. The skill we wanted to practice was to take possession, have poise, and get the puck out of our zone, and deep into theirs. You did that brilliantly. Now we have a new skill in our hockey toolbox for the remainder of the season.
>
> From now on, you should have confidence in this skill, and when we are scrambling near our goalie, you are tired, or don't know what to do with the puck and begin to panic; have some poise, take possession, and get it out of our zone. That is how you live to fight another day as a team.

TREAT GAMES AS YOUR PRIMARY CLASSROOM

But you learned something even more important this morning. You learned when you work together as a team, with everyone doing their respective jobs without excuses, you can have success. Today you were successful, and don't let anyone tell you differently!"

It is impossible to overstate how important the post-game talk is to reinforcing lifelong character traits like best effort, self-belief, and grit. Post-game is where you can reinforce these principles with fresh examples and open-minded players. **An effective coach recognizes there is always a lesson to be learned in every single game, regardless of the outcome**.

I have had hundreds of these teaching moments during my thirty-year coaching career and I have tried to take full advantage of every one of them. Here are a few abbreviated examples to help you conjure up some of your own thoughts on how to take advantage of this important coaching moment.

> "That was a gritty performance. When you believe and work together, these types of results are possible."

> "Tough loss. It stings and it should. But use it to fuel your fire to improve, not weigh you down. We will be better for this."

> "Remember, when you leave the locker room hold your heads up high. You gave your very best in pursuit, and that is all anyone can ever ask from you."

> "I asked you before the game to be able to look in the mirror and at your teammates knowing you gave your ultimate best today. I'm looking at you now and I can see you did. That is why you leave here successful!"

> "It never matters who we play, only how we play. You showed them what team-oriented, never-quit, and grit mean today."

Game day is one of the rare opportunities where an adult will have the undivided attention of their impressionable student-athletes. Use this experiential learning opportunity to teach your players something of value, or to reinforce the life lessons you want to inculcate. It is worth repeating. An effective coach treats game-day as their primary classroom in full recognition their players are more receptive to learning before, during, and immediately after a game.

TREAT GAMES AS YOUR PRIMARY CLASSROOM

Endnotes

19 Similar points about the long-term vision of teaching were made by Randy Pausch during his college lecture turned book entitled, *The Last Lecture*. This book is cited in the appendix.

20 Icing in hockey is when the puck moves from the defensive side of the mid-ice red line (mid-court), all the way to the opposite end of the ice or offensive zone, without being touched by a player. The referee stops play, and the puck is brough back to the offending team's defensive zone where play resumes on a face-off (tip-off).

21 In a sixty-minute game, it is estimated a professional hockey player only possesses the puck for a total of forty-five seconds or one percent of the total game time. Search topic online: *how much time does a hockey player touch the puck?* Reviewed February 2022.

22 In ice hockey, the "strong side" of the playing surface is where the puck is located, the "weak side" is where the puck is not located.

Conclusion

You can win over players and parents, and have fun too!

My favorite story about the power of teaching effort, belief, and grit to players, comes from a game my high-school team played a few seasons ago against our cross-town rivals. These games are always fun for the players because the arena is packed with raucous students from both schools.

Unfortunately, we found ourselves battling from behind the entire game. With around six minutes remaining in the game, our opponent scored a back-breaking goal to put us behind our 1 to their 4 goals. Our student fans started heading toward the exits, and as they did, I saw the players' heads drop toward the floor indicating they were giving up.

As a coach, you simply cannot let your players get used to giving up. Quitting can become a life habit like all others, which is why regardless of the score, opponent, obstacles, or insurmountable odds you may be facing, you have to keep fighting. This is an important life lesson and has nothing to do with the scoreboard. To make this point to the team I called my one-and-only time-out so the players could huddle up around me, and I could teach.

> "Listen. You know I don't care about the scoreboard. I care about your effort and attitude. We outwork our opponents, win or lose. And right now, you are not outworking them. You're not competing. We may not

win this game, but let's win the final six minutes. It's 0 to 0 in my book, outwork them in the final six. Win the last six minutes of this game!"

The team accepted the challenge and picked up their pace, and a minute after the time-out, we scored a goal off a rebound. The goal narrowed the deficit, but something more powerful happened too; the players started to believe they could come from behind and win.

With around three-minutes remaining in the game, our unrelenting attack forced our opponents to take a penalty. The power play and man-up advantage paid off for us, and we scored again making it our 3 to their 4 goals. Our team was now clearly outworking our opponents on both ends of the rink.

Down by one goal with one minute to play in the game, I waved our goalie over to the bench to add an extra attacker on the ice. By the way, an interesting dissonance happens when your goalie is pulled leaving your net wide open: time moves slowly and quickly all at the same time. Tick, tick, tick is all I heard as the clock winded down toward zero in my mind.

With about fifteen seconds remaining on the clock, our team moved the puck deep into the offensive end of the ice just behind the opposing goaltender. I watched as all six of my players battled for either possession or position in the game's final throws. In the corner, two of our players were battling for control of the puck, while in front of the goal, two of their teammates were fighting to evade the other team's defenders.

Inexplicably, at the exact same moment two of our team's players won their respective battles: one player behind the net secured the puck while his teammate in front

CONCLUSION

of the goal earned momentary space away from his pesky defender.

In the blink of an eye a connection was made, and an impeccable pass from behind the net was met by an equally impressive shot. With just thirteen seconds remaining in the contest, we scored to tie the game and send it into overtime!

I'm sure you figured it out by now, we ended up winning the game fifty seconds into sudden-death overtime thereby cementing the game as the most memorable come-from-behind victory in our program's twenty-five-year history.

This positive memory will be implanted in the minds of fifteen hockey players forever, constantly reminding them to always give their best effort, believe in themselves, and never, ever, give up. This is the culture of effective teams, effective coaches, and successful people.

This come-from-behind victory was a full-circle moment for me as a coach. Just three short seasons earlier our team was on the losing end of a similar game. Why the turnaround? Simply because the players embraced an alternate definition of success. A definition where your personal best effort, believing in yourself and your teammates, and persevering despite obstacles are much more important than a scoreboard result.

I penned this short blueprint for the rookie youth coach who accepted the voluntary position and immediately thought, "Now what?" And for the veteran coach looking for a fresh perspective, or perhaps even a reason to continue coaching. I am absolutely confident if you follow the coaching blueprint outlined in the preceding pages, you will give yourself an incredible head-start on your way to becoming a highly effective coach.

But more importantly, you will begin teaching lifelong

character traits through sports, and by doing so, perhaps change the trajectory of your players' lives. This in my mind, is how you truly win over your players and their parents.

I just ask you to remember a very important principle as you begin your coaching journey: remain player-centric by always putting the players' best interests above all else. Most, if not all of the players will conclude their competitive playing careers as they graduate from high school. However, the life lessons you teach them through the sport can elevate them forever.

As a player-centric coach, do not worry about the scoreboard, winning, or losing. Instead, motivate your players to do the only thing you can ever ask of anyone, to do their personal best. This is how you can teach them a can-do, never-quit attitude that will help them achieve whatever version of life success they ultimately define for themselves.

As you help the players learn, grow, and develop, make sure to set and manage realistic expectations as well as provide the players with honest feedback. A great way to do this is by leveraging the Gutt Check Performance Matrix as a central focus of your overall coaching philosophy. Trust me, it works.

Remember to always be a positive secondary role model to both the players and parents. Your young and impressionable players need and deserve this type of emotionally mature coach. So do their parents.

Your players want to learn your great sport, be competitive, and have fun. Take the time to proactively plan balanced practices to facilitate players' skills development, inspire teamwork, and prepare them to compete physically.

CONCLUSION

Finally, never forget the absolute best opportunity to teach your players life lessons will be on game days. Games are the fresh emotional experience a student-athlete needs to truly become more receptive to listening, understanding, and learning. Make sure to use this rare opportunity to maximum effect and teach or reinforce the character traits that will sustain your players long after their competitive playing days are done. Remember, there is a lesson to be learned in every single game; win or lose, lopsided or not.

If you called me up for some advice after volunteering to coach a youth team, the first thing I would tell you is to make sure the players hustle and have fun so they keep playing the sport year after year. Then I'd talk to you about the seven coaching recommendations contained in this book. But most importantly I'd tell you this: thank you!

Thank you for serving our communities by volunteering to coach. It is truly an honorable undertaking with an incredible higher-level purpose: helping your student-athletes begin to realize their life potential.

Thank you for teaching your players that being able to look in the mirror, or a loved one's eyes, knowing that working as hard as they could to become the best versions of themselves possible, is success.[23] It is all we can, or should, ever ask of anyone.

Thank you for starting the process to teach incredibly important character traits to your players through sports. Traits like grit, self-belief, and effort are the prerequisites to becoming the best possible you in life.

Thank you for continually pushing to become the best teacher, the best coach, and the best secondary adult role model you can for your impressionable youth players. Your student-athletes and their parents deserve your very best effort too.

Finally, thank you for taking the time to read this coaching blueprint. By doing so, I am confident you will become a much more effective youth coach, win over the players and their parents, and have fun too!

Just do me one favor as you move forward along your coaching journey: never forget how important you are to your student-athletes character development. You are making a huge positive difference, and our players and communities are better off because of you. I am forever grateful. Now, go get 'em!

If I do my full duty, the rest will take care of itself.
General George S. Patton, Jr. [24]

CONCLUSION

Endnotes

23 My abbreviated version of legendary Coach John Wooden's definition of success. See *Wooden: A lifetime of Observations and Reflections On and Off the Court.* This book is cited in the appendix and bibliography.

24 *Contrails.* Air Force Academy Cadet Handbook. This book is cited in the appendix and bibliography.

Afterword

"Coach," I answered catching my younger brothers by surprise. But then again, the question itself was unexpected after a round of golf, a few beers, and a lot of brotherly teasing.

My brothers had made the trek from Minnesota to Ohio ahead of the rest of the extended family. The next-day's informal family reunion was in celebration of my pending promotion to full Colonel in the United States Air Force. The honor to serve our nation and Airmen at this level of responsibility was a career goal of mine, and my relatives justifiably wanted to celebrate the occasion with my family and me.

My father, grandfather, step-father, two brothers, and several of my uncles were all veterans of the Armed Services, although none had made it a career. I'm pretty confident when this group of veterans received the promotion invitation from a four-star general, a Minnesota native himself, they felt compelled to attend the festivities fueled by a healthy dose of curiosity and disbelief.

When my Grandpa Gutterman found out his oldest grandson was being promoted to Colonel he was beyond ecstatic. Grandpa served as an Army Private in World War II for two years and saw action in both the Pacific and European theaters of war.

Our family would learn decades after the war about Grandpa's wartime experience in the Battle of the Hürtgen Forest, fought near the German-Belgium border. Determining who was a friend or foe in the dense German forest proved difficult for both sides, and after a skirmish Herman

HUSTLE AND HAVE FUN!

Gutterman was mistakenly captured by American soldiers and taken as their Prisoner of War. Grandpa shared the Americans felt anyone with a name like Herman Gutterman, must be a German spy in an American uniform! It took a few weeks for the American Forces to realize Herman Gutterman was an American soldier, after which he was sent back to the front lines.

I had the good fortune of both my parents, as-well-as Grandparents, being present for my graduation from the United States Air Force Academy 18 years earlier. After Grandpa, a retired truck driver, helped pin on my Second Lieutenant butter bars he said "only in America can a former Army Private pin officer rank onto his grandson's shoulders." My Dad, a Navy vet himself, said something similar while foreshadowing the result my graduation would have on the family lineage.

Grandpa would say something similar the day I pinned on the rank of Colonel, but this time with the preface, "If your dad was still alive." [25] My dad watched the promotion ceremony from heaven, and only I could hear his whispered pride.

The post-golf ribbing ended when my brother grabbed the pitcher of beer and started to refill the three empty glasses on the patio table overlooking the putting green. As he poured, he looked sideways at me and asked, "Greg, would you rather be called coach or general?"

His inquiry was brilliantly difficult for me to answer because he knew full well it targeted two of my three life passions: my Air Force and my student-athletes (my family begins the triad). My brother reasoned since I was about to pin on the rank of colonel in the Profession of Arms, I'd want to climb one more rung of the military ladder to become a "one-star" brigadier general.

He also knew my "how I got here" story, started with the fact I lucked into a career in the Air Force only because I was recruited to play college hockey at the Air Force Academy. The Academy led me to Utah, where the high school and college teams I coached won a state championship and four consecutive bids to the college club-level national tournament, respectively. With a hockey coaching pedigree like this, my brother thought I had an interest in becoming a high-end hockey coach someday too.

I did my best to change the subject and avoid answering this complicated question altogether. But the fact both brothers had experience playing and coaching ice hockey, and both were Air Force Veterans themselves, made escape impossible.

After as-long-a-delay as they would tolerate, he asked the question again. "Come on Greg, seriously, would you rather be called coach or general?"

"Well, if I have to pick one, then coach," I answered

"That's bullshit!" my brothers echoed in stereo.

My youngest brother, who had sat smiling and listening to his oldest brother's interrogation, took a drink of his beer, looked right at me, and asked "Why?"

Now don't get me wrong. I loved every minute of my professional military career providing war-winning capabilities to our Nation's Airmen. I was involved in research, development, test, and evaluation efforts on key weapon systems, engines, aircraft, communications, business systems, and even served as an international arms broker for a while. My roles in the Air Force were exciting, challenging, purpose-filled, and rewarding, and I would sign up to do it all again in a single heartbeat.

The Air Force military, civilian, and contractor team has the noblest of all missions, and the threats they face are never-ending. The pride I have supporting this incredibly important higher-level purpose is amplified by the fulfillment I feel having been a small part of the world's best military team. A large globally dispersed and diverse team of Airmen who share important life values like integrity, service, and excellence. I'm so damn proud to have been on the Air Force Team for thirty-four years and continue to be grateful for our nation's amazing military patriots who, day in and day out, accomplish amazing work in defense of our freedoms.

I grabbed my glass of barley, hops and water, and took an intentionally long sip to buy some time before answering my youngest brother's "why" question.

"Well," I said, "I love my Air Force, my teammates, and the higher-level purpose of protecting our way of life. That's why I've made it a career. Quite frankly I'd do it again in the blink of an eye. But when people are asked, who influenced you the most while you were growing up? They won't answer General Gutterman. But they may, someday, answer Coach Gutterman. Generals are accorded trust and respect; coaches have to earn it daily."

People who achieve greatness in life are often asked "Who was the one person that positively influenced you the most growing up?" They answer by telling us about a mentor who pushed, challenged, and motivated them. A person who believed in them and helped them believe in themselves. A role model that held them personally accountable for their actions or inactions. And more times than not, this person is a teacher or coach.

This is why being a youth coach is such an incredible

AFTERWORD

responsibility: you have an opportunity to positively impact a player for life! This book stemmed from my hope that your youth players will someday answer that question by naming you.

Endnotes

---

25 I arranged for Grandpa to stay in a Distinguished Visitor (DV) suite on Wright-Patterson Air Force Base with my uncle, who served as his driver for the long promotion-weekend celebration. I saw them soon after they checked into the suite, and Grandpa had this wide smile on his face. The guestbook in the room was filled with colonels and generals' names. "So I signed it *Private* Gutterman," he said laughing.

Appendix A: Coaching Commitment

gut check (noun)

a test or assessment of courage, character, or determination. (Source: Merriam-Webster Dictionary Online)

Gutt Check™

1. Leverage decades of experience and education to reflectively determine the most effective methods for accomplishing meaningful duties.

2. Coach Gutterman's nickname and a reference to his favorite sport, hockey.

Gutt Check: Remain Player Centric

Identify your favorite role model (or two) growing up.

List three reasons why they were your favorite role model.

Complete this statement: "I coach to (or because) _____."

Gutt Check: Don't Worry About the Scoreboard

Consider a significant disappointment you encountered (or witnessed).

List a few reasons why you felt satisfied or dissatisfied with the way you handled the situation.

Complete this statement: "During the season, I want to teach the players to _____."

Gutt Check: Manage Expectations

Think about a time in your life when you received constructive (even brutal) feedback.

Identify why the feedback was of value to you.

Complete this statement: "I will provide positive and constructive feedback to the players by _____."

Gutt Check: Act Like the Role Model You Are

Recall a difficult event, situation, or conversation you had in the past.

List the reasons the difficult event, situation, or conversation went well (or did not go well).

Complete this statement: "I will control my emotions and set a positive tone for my players and team, by _____."

Gutt Check: Treat the Parent's Like Adults

Complete this statement: "The three things a parent can do to help you as a coach are _____."

Use the three things from above to create your parental communication rule set or to establish your healthy boundaries.

Set a date for a pre-season meeting with the players and their parents to discuss your coaching philosophy and communication rule set.

Gutt Check: Run Balanced Practices

Review the USA Hockey American Development Model practice plans for your players age group at https://www.admkids.com (website current as of August 2022). These are great practice plans for all sports coaches to leverage or learn from.

Determine 3 key skills to practice, 3 team plays to practice, a small area fun competitive game to play, and a competitive conditioning drill. This is done before every practice.

Proactively write down your one-hour balanced practice plan.
- Warm-up and stretching (5 minutes)
- Three five-minute skills stations (15 minutes)
- Three five-minute progressively building team plays (15 minutes)

HUSTLE AND HAVE FUN!

- Small area competitive fun game for max repetitions (10 minutes)
- Competition based conditioning drills (7 minutes)
- Free play for fun or to work on their own (5 minutes)

Gutt Check: Treat Games as Your Primary Classroom

Identify and communicate to the players three to five "keys to the game" before warm-ups begin. (e.g. communication, effort, have fun!)

Before the game, remind all coaches to teach the players on the bench instead of directing traffic on the ice (field, or court).

Proactively develop your post-game teaching point(s). Emphasize these before the game, during the game, and especially after the game when players are more receptive to learning.

Gutt Check: Coaching Commitment

On a three-by-five-inch index card write down the five coaching statements from above. This is your baseline coaching commitment.

1) I coach to (or because) _____.
2) During the season, I want to teach the players to _____.
3) I will provide positive and constructive feedback to the players by _____.
4) I will control my emotions and set a positive tone for my players and team, by _____.

COACHING COMMITMENT

5) The three most influential people in your players lives are _____.

Place the index card in your pocket and review it often.

Appendix B: Playbook

I recommend coaches write down their coaching philosophy to provide a foundation from which to teach. This will also help you remain emotionally centered and more effectively set and manage expectations with players and their parents.

Your playbook should include several sections such as your personal coaching statement or why you coach, team and player expectations or culture, team plays, and team rules as a minimum. Here's an example from my 2016 high school team playbook.

Coaching Philosophy

I coach to give back, to teach life lessons, and to help you succeed. Everything I have today is based on the life lessons and character traits I learned playing team sports, especially hockey.

Discipline, grit, teamwork, personal responsibility, self-belief, self-control, trust, humility, and gratitude--these are the character traits of successful people and successful teams.

My philosophy is summed up in a simple phrase: personal goals are met through hard work. I contend working hard for results and improvement is the key to success as you, not your parents, peers, coaches, or teachers, define it.

HUSTLE AND HAVE FUN!

Team Culture

Hard work, giving your personal best effort toward improvement to meet your goals, without excuses, is the key to success. Hard work toward achieving results, not the scoreboard, defines our team.

Remember this diagram...it will be used time and again.

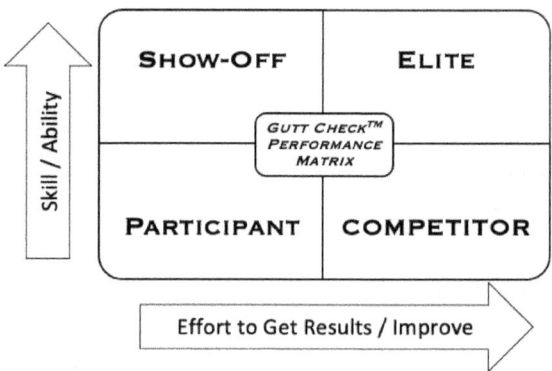

If you feel you are not getting enough game time, I'll ask you: where are you on this diagram during games and practices? You get what you earn – through hard work – earn it, compete!

I want you to be a competitor by always bringing your personal best effort in everything you do: games, practices, on/off ice, education, jobs, and more. Giving your best effort in everything you undertake is a personal investment in your future. Invest in yourself to reach your full potential by working hard to get better, every day.

Team Plays

This is the traditional "playbook" section which should include descriptions and diagrams of the team plays you plan to implement.

The majority of young athletes are visual learners, so I also recommend including links to online videos of your team plays so the players can watch them in action for deeper understanding.

Team Rules

This is where you put in your expectations on behavioral values and norms for your team. This section includes your team's rules (e.g. be respectful, be on time), expectations (e.g. be a good teammate), and definition of success (e.g. best effort and attitude).

Appendix C: Videos and Books

Recommended Viewing and Reading List

Videos

The following videos are widely available online. The links cited below were current as of December 2021.

Angela Duckworth on Grit: "Grit! The Power of Passion and Perseverance: Angela Duckworth." https://youtu.be/H14bBuluwB8

Growth Mindset vs Fixed Mindset animation. https://www.youtube.com/watch?v=KUWn_TJTrnU&t=54s

John Wooden on Success: "The Difference Between Winning and Succeeding." https://youtu.be/0MM-psvqiG8

Books

Discover your True North. Bill George. John Wiley and Sons, Inc. Hoboken, NJ. 2015.

Grit: The Power of Passion and Perseverance. Angela Duckworth. Scribner. New York. 2016.

Leaders Eat Last: Why Some Teams Pull Together and Others Don't. Simon Sinek. Portfolio / Penguin. Penguin Group. New York, NY. 2014

Leading with the Heart: Coach K's Successful Strategies for Basketball, Business, and Life. Mike Krzyzewski and Donald T. Phillips. Hachette Book Group. New York, NY. 2000.

Mindset: The New Psychology of Success, how we can learn to fulfill our potential. Dweck, Carol S. Ph.D. Ballantine Books Trade Paperback Edition 2016/

Outliers: The Story of Success. Malcolm Gladwell. Allen Lane, Penguin Books. 2008

Primal Leadership Learning to Lead with Emotional Intelligence. Richard Boyatzis and Annie McKee. Harvard Business School Press. 2002

The Last Lecture. Randy Pausch, with Jeffrey Zaslow. Hyperion. New York. 2008.

The 7 Habits of Highly Effective People: Powerful Lessons in Personal Change. Stephen R. Covey. Simon and Schuster, New York, NY. 2004.

Winning Every Day: The Game Plan for Success. Lou Holtz. HarperCollins Publishers Inc., New York, NY. 1999

VIDEOS AND BOOKS

Win Forever: Live, Work, and Play Like a Champion. Pete Carrol with Yogi Roth and Kristoffer A. Garin. Portfolio-Penguin. 2010

Wooden: A Lifetime of Observations and Reflections On and Off the Court. Coach John Wooden. McGraw Hill. 1997.

Wooden on Leadership: How to Create a Winning Organization. John Wooden and Steve Jamison. McGraw-Hill. 2009

Bibliography

Contrails. Air Force Academy Cadet Handbook. Volume 31. The United States Air Force Academy, Colorado. 1985-1986.

Leonard, Steven Matthew. *Channeling Controversy: 10 Patton Quotes That Define Good Leadership*, Mar 2, 2021. Clearancejobs.com. Reviewed October 2021.

Outliers: The Story of Success. Malcolm Gladwell. Allen Lane, Penguin Books. 2008

Wooden, John. Wooden: *A Lifetime of Observations and Reflections On and Off the Court*. Coach John Wooden. McGraw Hill. 1997.

Acknowledgments

First and foremost, my family, Leslie, and the kids. You are my oxygen and my reason for everything.

Mom and Dad. Despite your escape from earthly bonds, I see the lessons you taught me clearer every day.

My youth Coaches. Thank you for focusing on my personal development in sports and life. You put me on the right path!

My mentors and advocates. You boosted me along the way, thank you!

My Air Force. I am grateful beyond belief to have been a small part of the world's most feared and respected fighting force.

My Editor and Reviewers. A debt of gratitude I will be unable to repay for all your thoughts, comments, and edits. Thank you for helping to make this book a reality.

Finally, my student-athletes. You are people of character who made me a better coach and person every day. Now get out there and use that team-oriented, never-quit, gritty attitude to build a successful life for yourselves!

Upcoming Books and Contact Information

Look for future Gutt Check™ series books by Coach-General Gutterman on the topics of leadership success, winning in bureaucracies, and more.

For information, workshops, speaking engagements, and more contact Coach Gutterman at CoachGutt@HustleandHave.Fun.

See more on Coach Gutterman's not-for-profit interest at Academyhockey.org.

About the Author

Brigadier General Greg Gutterman, United States Air Force retired, is a native of Minnesota where he grew up playing baseball, football, and ice hockey. He played National Collegiate Athletic Association Division I ice hockey at the United States Air Force Academy and subsequently served our nation for 30 years as an active-duty military officer. General Gutterman's official biography is available online.

During his military career, Coach Gutterman accumulated three decades of coaching experience. He has coached players from three-year-old to college-aged players across six states during his military assignments. He is President of the not-for-profit Academy Hockey Club and was named a 2021 finalist for the National Hockey League's Stick Tap for Service Award.

www.ingramcontent.com/pod-product-compliance
Lightning Source LLC
Chambersburg PA
CBHW071519040426
42444CB00008B/1718